BEAR IN THE BULLRING

BEAR IN THE BULLRING

How Independent Thinking Protects Your Money & Improves Your Life

DAVID ROSENBERG

sh.
SUTHERLAND HOUSE

TORONTO, 2026

Sutherland House
416 Moore Ave., Suite 304
Toronto, ON M4G 1C9

First edition, September 2026

If you are interested in inviting one of our authors to a live event or media appearance, please contact sranasinghe@sutherlandhousebooks.com and visit our website at sutherlandhousebooks.com for more information about our authors and their schedules.

We acknowledge the support of the Government of Canada.

Manufactured in China

Library and Archives Canada Cataloguing in Publication
Title: Bear in the bullring : how independent thinking protects your money & improves your life / David Rosenberg.
Names: Rosenberg, David (Economist), editor.
Description: First edition.
Identifiers: Canadiana (print) 20260196649 | Canadiana (ebook) 20260196657 | ISBN 9781997701774 (hardcover) | ISBN 9781997701781 (EPUB)
Subjects: LCSH: Investments—Decision making. | LCSH: Business cycles. | LCSH: Financial risk management. | LCSH: Finance, Personal.
Classification: LCC HG4521 .R67 2026 | DDC 332.6—dc23

ISBN 978-1-997701-77-4
eBook 978-1-997701-78-1

Contents

INTRODUCTION

How a Bear Survived in the Bullring

This is not a conventional "how to invest" book. That is because there has never been anything in my forty-year career as an economist and strategist that can be remotely described as conventional. This is more a guide based on the life experiences, personal and commercial, that helped shape my approach toward forecasting and investing. It is about how to make money and save money without being blindly bullish on the market at all times.

Life has taught me that the keys to success reside in daring to be different: to be unique and differentiated; to avoid following the herd, being a linear thinker, and embracing the consensus view.

When I was in my mid-twenties, I read Charles Mackay's 1841 classic *Extraordinary Popular Delusions and the Madness of Crowds.* It had a tremendous impact on my approach to investing and helped me and those who heeded my advice avoid the pitfalls of the severe bear markets of 1990, 2001–2002, and 2007–2009. You can read in later chapters about the intense pressure I was under at Merrill Lynch to change my views on the markets in the summer of 2007, right as the housing bubble was getting set to burst. It's a miracle I wasn't fired, but the reality is that me and my economics team at the time were churning out phenomenal and unique research. There is no substitute for producing excellent analytical thought, whether or not you are on the wrong side of the trade at a particular point of time.

For those who advocate a "buy and hold" investment strategy, I have news for you. Not participating in bear markets over the past five decades would have meant that your equity portfolio would be 50 percent bigger today as a result. And that is my stock-in-trade: keeping investors out of trouble. Even in my Gluskin Sheff era, when I also was under pressure to be bullish at all times, the sales team would advertise me to clients as being a combination of "brake lights and turn indicators." That car analogy is 100 percent correct. Would you really want to drive without your brake lights or right-and-left-turn indicators? I think not. What I find most interesting is how most investors actually treat their vehicles with more care than they do their portfolios, which they typically want to run with high-octane gas.

And if that earns me the label of being a "perma bear," it's only that—a label. A label perpetuated by the media for the most part, and this one has stuck to me for most of my career. When I did turn bullish from 2012 to 2017, there were a lot of people who simply refused to believe it!

Once a label is established, it sticks. So be it. The simple truth is that nobody can be a perma anything because nothing in life is permanent. I get this label only because I have spent a career preaching diversification, capital preservation, and a strategy of building wealth prudently over time as opposed to get-rich-quick philosophies that help make you friends in this business but inevitably lose you money. I firmly believe that winning means not losing. Especially when it comes to your savings.

This perma bear, as an aside, has lost money in the market just one year over the past four decades, in 1987 amidst the October collapse. That was a lesson discussed in this book, which is to not fear making mistakes, but to learn from them and don't make the same one twice.

It was more than a century after the publication of *Extraordinary Popular Delusions and the Madness of Crowds* that Merrill Lynch's venerable technical strategist (and my role model) Bob Farrell pioneered the incorporation of investor sentiment in equity market strategy. This makes sense since "animal spirits" measured by the shifts in the market multiple vastly outweigh earnings fundamentals at any point across the investment cycle, and that holds in both bull and bear markets.

My life experiences are something I want to share because they show the value of having courage in your convictions, in thinking not of what the headlines will read today or tomorrow, but what they will be saying six months, a year, and even a decade from now, in resisting pressures from your superiors to change your view when you have high conviction, in daring to be different by not following the herd mentality, and in not succumbing to fear, which is an obstacle to effective decision-making. I am not sure this is well-known, but the most oft-used commandment from God cited in the Torah is *"al tira,"* or fear not. These all are the critical ingredients to success, not just in your professional life, but in your personal life.

One of my lasting memories of my time at Merrill Lynch was a high-net-worth event at one of the hotels in midtown Manhattan. This was in my final few months at the firm, in early 2009, as the brutal bear market was entering its final stages. The story says a lot about the gap that exists between investor perception and reality. I spoke at the event, and as I was talking to clients in the lobby after, this elderly woman, likely well into her eighties or even nineties and impeccably dressed, walks up to me, shakes my hand, and says, "Mr. Rosenberg, you really surprised me." I told her that only my kids call me Mr. Rosenberg and she could feel free to call me Dave. I asked what surprised her.

"Well," she said, "I was surprised because you were so funny and you seem like such a nice man."

"Why would you think otherwise?"

"Oh, well, it's because you're so bearish."

"Madam," I said, touching her arm warmly, "that is my market view, not my personality."

I get similar remarks to this day. Some people must think I'm a troll living under a bridge. Or a bear in a cave, as if anyone in this business who doesn't promote a bullish narrative must forage for salmon and berries.

* * *

I've been asked why, at the spry age of sixty-five, I decided to write my first book. It's a legitimate question, and it comes on the heels of years of clients, friends, and colleagues in the industry asking why I had not yet published a book. The requests started to accumulate in 2009 when, after seven years in the Wall Street jungle, I left my perch as chief economist at Merrill Lynch and came home to Toronto.

I considered publishing a book then. The challenge was figuring out what it should be about. I could have written about the Great Financial Crisis, since I was there on the frontlines and called the recession and the housing market meltdown, although I must admit that things turned out to be far worse than I ever imagined, and I never would have thought that Mother Merrill would have to be bought out by another major bank. But those types of books on the causes and consequences of the Great Financial Crisis are a dime a dozen. Why beat a dead horse (as horrible a thought as that is)?

In the spring of 2009, I ended up at Gluskin Sheff, at the time a well-respected and swanky boutique fund manager in Toronto. I was chief economist and strategist. Two epiphanies at Gluskin Sheff helped me answer the question of what my book should be about. First, I had the opportunity early in my tenure at Gluskin Sheff to share a platform at a client event with Ira Gluskin, who was CIO and a legendary investor in Canada. Just before I headed to the podium, Ira said, "Dave, put away your slides and just go up to the lectern and talk about your life experiences and how they have shaped your overall market views and philosophy." I had to pivot and do something out of my comfort zone. But I was struck by how well my off-the-cuff, straight-from-the-heart speech was received. That sort of presentation, as opposed to a canned slide show, was far more effective in keeping the crowd awake. Thanks to Ira for that lesson—it was a game-changer for me.

Second, I was contacted by a major publishing house in Toronto out of the blue in 2010. It wanted me to write a book exactly as I described earlier. Life's lessons and how they informed my craft as a market seer. Over the span of six months, I met with the publisher's team, outlining chapters for this proposed book. I had a title for it, "*Talking to the Wall*," with a picture of Wall and Broad Streets on the front cover. Prior to each meeting, I notified the senior management team at Gluskin Sheff (the two founders had by now sold down their shares and stepped aside). I knew that there was no way I could publish a book without approval from my superiors. They knew that I was involved in discussions, but expressed no interest. The senior folks at the publishing company were astonished that nobody from Gluskin Sheff came to the meetings. After our last meeting, when I was given a contract, the new management at Gluskin Sheff sprang into action. I'd sent out an email at 4:00 p.m. saying that I had a contract in hand and that if I did not receive approval by 5:00 p.m., I would take that as a thumbs-up and would sign it. By 4:15 p.m., I got an in-person response that went something like this: "Dave, we are struggling with redemptions and our investment returns have been subpar recently, and we fear that clients will wonder why it is that David Rosenberg, in his first year at the firm, is deciding to write a book instead of dedicating all his time towards steering the investment team in the right direction."

"So, no to this book deal?" I asked.

"No book deal," I was told.

I understood the sensitivity. What I didn't understand is why they waited until the last second to instruct me not to write the book. So much time and resources wasted.

Still, my eleven-year tenure at Gluskin Sheff gave me experience in wealth management, taught me how to be relevant to an investor putting money on the line, and how to distill ideas and communicate effectively to a retail client base. It was a perfect blend of "buy side" experience to go with my decades of experience as a big-name economist and strategist at big banks, or what is called the "sell side." Positioned at a boutique wealth manager, I was able to receive all the Wall Street and Bay Street research from my former competitors and, truth be told, it all sounded the same. They all hugged the consensus. Going against the herd in the forecasting business takes courage. You are risking your career. Your superiors will rarely tolerate a differentiated view. As a result, practically all sell-side macro research is a commodity, something I spent much of my professional life trying to avoid. It is a miracle that I never got fired, because I was a pain in the ass for many of my former bosses for not toeing the line. I never succumbed to pressure to change my view from the C-suite, although I experienced a whole lot of resistance. And I came away from Gluskin Sheff knowing that I didn't want to write the kind of book that picked over the Great Financial Crisis and the demise of Mother Merrill.

I had long dreamed of a day when I'd be ready to set up my own shop and not have to push product or pull punches for my employers. That dream came true in January 2020 when I decided to hang up my own shingle, starting a firm devoted to publishing unbiased research with independent thought. I tell my clients what I am detecting, what I am seeing that is about to happen around the bend, and what I am doing. I never tell people what to do. It's up to them—we are all grown-ups. In retrospect, Rosenberg Research was always going to happen. It was just a matter of the timing.

Much like this book. I knew I'd do it at some point. I had it in mind that I would not write a book about how to invest, or delve into the causes of financial crises, or the blunders of monetary and fiscal policymakers.

There are many of those books available. I'd spent a career stressing the importance of being unique and differentiated, and most "how to" books are basically commodities, like Wall Street research reports. Recently, I talked with a major US publisher. It wanted a manuscript that told people how to invest for the future. To which I said, and I meant no disrespect, if that is what you want from me, subscribe to my newsletter. It incorporates my highest conviction market views.

What I've put in this book is more important than transitory advice on what stocks to buy today. It is timeless advice. It is the sum of the learnings and experiences that have shaped my economic and investment views. It offers guidance on how to respond to the pressures, challenges, opportunities, and obstacles that life inevitably throws at you, both personally and financially. It is designed to help you cut through the fog, focus on what's important, make strong decisions, and take your success to a higher level. Those are the purposes of this book. It may be full of stories, and echo the casual, off-the-cuff speech I gave at Ira's suggestion, but it has serious intent.

* * *

Experience and a long-term view are more important in today's investment environment than ever before. The financial industry is loaded with people who couldn't care less about their clients and have no concept of risk. To many advisors, client service boils down to golf games and remembering your kids' birthdays. Optimal portfolio construction, capital preservation, and risk mitigation strategies are relics of the past. These fund managers want only a positive narrative to keep clients engaged in their highest fee products. That is why perma bulls will always be gainfully employed—why those economists and strategists who missed the mega bubbles in 2000 and 2007 can still be found today espousing the same messages in what is the third most acute maniacal period of the past century.

Someone talking about or identifying tail risks, the danger of extreme and rare events, in bullish markets spoils their party. I delivered a boardroom presentation to a group of financial advisors at a major bank just a few months ago. When I invoked Warren Buffett and Jeremy Grantham, one of the younger attendees interrupted me to ask why anyone would ever heed the advice of old, tired, out-of-touch men in a new AI-driven era of wealth creation. When I responded that experience never goes out of style, he rolled his eyes and chuckled.

My son and COO, Jacob, was at a cocktail party where he was introduced to another thirty-something advisor. When this advisor discovered where Jacob worked, he said, "tell your father that I have a message for him—he is a fool." My business has been successful, but I cannot count the number of subscribers who have canceled over these past six years, not because of poor quality research, not because of poor client service, but because I wasn't bullish enough for them.

I recently had lunch with an advisor (and friend) who is a client of mine. He is at a big Canadian bank and told me one of the branches invited one of my prime competitors in from New York for a client lunch in Toronto. When I asked why I had never been invited in to chat with this group of advisors, I was told, "Rosie, you simply don't have a bullish view of the S&P 500 so there is no chance they will ever ask you in." A bullish view. That's what it takes. The market for insightful analysis has taken a back seat to the positivity of your market outlook. It's a bear market for deep thought. The fact that there are so few of us in this industry absent a constant bullish bias should mean our work is more valuable—we're a scarce resource!

I believe in Mother Nature, I believe that cycles exist, and like my hero, Bob Farrell, I don't believe in new eras or periods of permanent excess. When I hear that we are living through a repeat of the Roaring Twenties, I remind people that the 1920s saw three separate recessions and ended with a burst bubble of historical proportions.

Investor behavior has changed enormously since I started in the financial industry in the mid-1980s. Gone are the days when people read in-depth research reports. What investors crave today are soundbites. They want quick, actionable advice. They want to be spoon-fed. They don't want to do any work. They would have no patience for the deep thinkers of years gone by: Hank Herrmann at Waddell & Reed, Jack Rivkin at Neuberger Berman, Paul McCulley at PIMCO, or Dick Hoey at Dreyfus.

Social media has had much to do with this. It has sapped the attention span of a generation of young portfolio managers and retail investors. It has fueled the proliferation of Robinhood accounts and Reddit communities. All with the aim of investing or trading with short-term mentalities.

Something tells me this is not just a product of social media and the digital age, but also of the world's central banks, especially the Federal Reserve, which has managed to convince investors that every correction will be met with both aggressive interest rate cuts and expanded balance sheets. It is incredible that the Fed's balance sheet today is three times the size it was at the peak of the 2008–09 financial crisis and the Great Recession, even though there is no crisis or recession (at least not yet).

The mantra of the "Fed put," coupled with the presence of Donald Trump, king of the risk-on trade, has nurtured this era of super-sized investor complacency. This is why the S&P 500 multiple, by almost any measure, is in the most expensive 5 percent zone of recorded history. The multiple is always the pulse of investor sentiment, and if it ever does embark on a classic Bob Farrell Rule #1 "mean reversion" process, we could see a pullback of more than 20 percent without any movement in corporate earnings.

It used to be that earnings growth drove bull markets. The multiple was fairly stable. In recent cycles, nearly half the bull markets we have experienced have been dominated by "animal spirits" that dictate expansions in price/earnings multiples. It's important to remember that in bear markets, the proverbial "elevator down," the multiple compression accounts for

80 percent of the drawdown. That is the power of emotion in this business, and that is what makes the current environment so different from when there was more rationality, discipline, and resolve in the industry.

Another very big change, especially this cycle, has been how "diversification" has become a dirty word. Never mind that having exposure to Treasuries in the classic 60/40 stock–bond asset mix during the Great Financial Crisis, cut the damage to your portfolio by half. The same held true in the 2000–2002 market meltdown, when equity returns nosedived nearly 50 percent and bond returns were positive to the tune of over 30 percent. A 60/40 stock–bond diversified asset mix meant your portfolio was hit two-thirds less hard than if you were "all in" on the S&P 500. This may not resonate much with those in their twenties and thirties, since time is on their side. They can much better withstand a classic bear market. The rest of us, especially in the baby boomer cohort, where the median age just hit seventy, should consider that in any plain-vanilla bear market, 80 percent of the prior bull market gains get wiped out. Diversification remains a prudent strategy.

It is not a well-advertised fact that the equity market has actually lost you money over a five-year interval no fewer than three times in the past two decades. The Treasury market has never done that. It is a ballast and a stabilizer in the portfolio. There is inflation risk and duration risk in Treasuries, to be sure, but they are unique in their payment safety characteristics. They are the only assets where certainty of payment is assured and guaranteed. It's the only thing you can buy where you know exactly how much money you will have thirty years from now.

I guess that makes me one of the last people in the financial industry not willing to play the game of dancing till the music stops. You can accuse me of not changing with the times. Criticism accepted. But I have always believed in diversification, portfolio rebalancing, resisting temptation, and patience. It was the tortoise, at the end of the story, who won the race.

It is my hope that my experiences as a perma bear—someone who not only survived but thrived in an industry that is once again drowning in bullish narratives—will help readers navigate both today's extremes and the certain challenges of years to come.

CHAPTER 1

Born into a Crisis

My very first day as a street economist came on October 19, 1987, the day of the great crash. Black Monday. Virtually everyone who knows me is aware of that. It was my first day as the financial economist at the Bank of Nova Scotia, and I was greener than green. But what a lesson.

On that first day, Aron Gampel, to whom I reported, called me into his office. The stock markets were collapsing globally and bond yields were tumbling sharply. I had barely been in my office for a minute, and was barely in his for ten seconds before he asked, "Can you go to the Telerate machine and tell me what the dollar is doing?" He needed that information ahead of the morning meetings on the trading floor. I had no idea what a Telerate was. It turned out to be the poor man's version of the Bloomberg terminals everyone in this business uses intensively today, and we all shared one Telerate in the department.

"You want me to come back to you with what the Canadian dollar is doing, right?"

He looked up at me from his desk, his eyes rolling, and screamed, "Not the Canadian dollar! The US dollar! If I wanted the Canadian dollar, I would have said Canadian dollar. In this business, when someone says, 'the dollar' there is only one dollar, and it is the US dollar!"

He didn't add "you big dummy!" but he may as well have.

I returned to Aron's office with the information on "the dollar," and he asked me, "What papers do you read in the morning?" I said, the *Globe and Mail* and *Financial Post*.

He was unimpressed. "Start adding the *Wall Street Journal, New York Times,* and *Financial Times* to your daily repertoire."

He then asked, "Do you read *Barron's* over the weekend?"

The truth was I'd never heard of *Barron's*, the venerable financial paper, published every Friday at the end of the trading week. At risk of embarrassment, I simply answered, "No, I don't."

I should add that he was reading the latest *Barron's* as we were talking. "I'm going to give you some important advice on your first day," he said. "Read, read, and read. And don't bother coming into the office on Monday morning if you haven't read *Barron's*." He then opened the paper to the inside page and pointed, "especially this part." Aron had his finger on "Up and Down Wall Street," a column penned by the greatest financial journalist of all time, Alan Abelson.

Of course, editions of the *Wall Street Journal,* the *New York Times*, and *Financial Times* also came out over the weekend. And while they were all delivered to the economics department at the bank, Aron was the one who got to read those copies first. I was making barely more than minimum wage. The Bank of Nova Scotia was renowned for being ultra-frugal. Not only were there no bonuses, I endured a salary freeze for three years in the early 1990s when Canadian inflation was running rampant, in large part because of the introduction of the hated Goods and Services Tax. The cost of these four newspapers was prohibitive. Getting fired was never an option for me, so I developed survival skills.

I would go on Saturdays to the local Lichtman's News and Books, a local icon from 1909 to 2000. I would head to the back of the store where the newspapers were, pen and pad of paper in hand, and read all the papers over two hours, one at a time, taking notes, keeping an eye out for the store manager, and then putting them back on the shelf. Thank the lord that the newspaper section was at the back of the store. I was never once busted in seven years. When I was hired by Sherry Cooper at BMO Nesbitt Burns in 1994, I received enough of a pay bump that I could drop this embarrassing behavior.

I have always been driven. I talk about the need to ensure you have balance in your life, but it has been a challenge for me. On my honeymoon in June 1991, I was running around Amsterdam to find the *Economist, Businessweek, Wall Street Journal, Barron's*, and the *Financial Times* because I knew that Aron Gampel was going on vacation the day I got back and I would be on the hook for the morning meetings. Romance gave way to reading. Over time, I figured it out.

Reading voraciously has held me in good stead. I was never smarter than any other economist or strategist, but nobody worked harder and nobody read more. I realized that when I referenced something that was going on somewhere in the world during a client meeting or a speech, people thought I was smart. All it meant was that I was informed. Information is power. Nobody knew this better than Don Coxe, the former strategy advisor at BMO, who could invariably weave into his conversation much more than the daily papers and journals—the works of Shakespeare and Greek tragedies. There was no one like Don, and those who were fortunate to hear him speak when he was in his prime know precisely what it is I am talking about.

I could never have guessed on that first day in October 1987 that I would go from not recognizing Alan Abelson's name to receiving space in his weekly column once he started reading my material after I joined Merrill Lynch in the 2000s. I remember the very first time he quoted my commentary extensively, sometime around 2005, on the beginning of the bubble in the US housing sector. It was a massive shot in the arm for my credibility. I started getting calls for lunch from Wall Street CIOs. None other than Henry Kaufman, who led the research team at Salomon

Brothers to great heights in the 1970s and 1980s, took me to lunch at his private club. Henry was then known as "Dr. Doom," which sounds a lot more dangerous than "perma bear." When we sat down to eat, the first thing he said was, "Anyone who gets quoted like you did in Alan's column is someone I want to meet."

A writer of extraordinary gifts, Alan Abelson produced "Up and Down Wall Street" for a half century. I would be blessed to become friends with him in his later years. He passed in May 2013. If you read his eulogies, you'd notice that so many people in financial markets thanked him for providing a positive inflection point in their careers.

Barron's, along with the other newspapers I mentioned earlier, and many more besides, has been one of the constants of my career. To this day, I get up at 4:15 a.m. in order to check the news and get my market newsletter out by 7:30 a.m. It all starts with reading.

I spent the rest of that first day, October 19, 1987, amid mayhem and pandemonium. It was a terrific lesson for a budding street economist. I followed my superiors, chief economist Bill Mackness, assistant chief economist Warren Jestin, and my direct boss and head of financial markets Aron Gampel, all day long as we moved around the trading floor and through the executive offices. I met all the senior people at the bank, including Cedric Ritchie, Gordon Bell, Peter Godsoe, and Bob Brooks—literally a who's who of Canadian banking. These people had ice in their veins. I had a pit in my stomach. I learned fast what it meant to keep a cool head as others lost theirs. The unforgettable images from that day of what happened in markets when the spell of bullishness finally breaks have always stood me in good stead.

CHAPTER 2

Let Your Passion Follow You

I took my first economics course as an eleventh-grade student at Hillcrest High School in Ottawa, back in 1976. I signed up for the course on a whim. I had zero clue what economics was about, but it sounded intriguing.

After my first day, I got home and Dad asked me, "So how was your Economics course today?"

"Dad," I said, "we learned about the classic Keynesian model that assumes no government."

"No government?" he said incredulously. He showed me his latest pay stub and how the federal government took more than half his gross pay (the top marginal tax rate in Canada kicks in at an egregiously low level). "Maybe find something a little more practical than economics."

So, I took Dad's advice and dropped economics, at the ripe young age of sixteen. I switched to a course in dramatic arts. It would actually be more valuable to me in the future. After all, so much of what economists in my business do is provide infotainment—a flair for the dramatic never hurts, so long as you don't overdo it and also provide the crowd with intelligence it can benefit from.

I owe my good grades in high school to my tenth-grade English and history teacher, Norbert Hyba. He made education an exciting experience for me, and my marks shot up after eons of below-average performance.

I grew up with three older siblings who were scholastically gifted, and I remember my ninth-grade homeroom teacher asking me, after reviewing my first report card, "Are you sure you're a Rosenberg?" From tenth gade on, I went from C's and D's to A's and B-pluses. Thanks, Mr. Hyba. I think teachers should be compelled to take courses in effective communication, because the ones who excel on that front are few and far between.

When it came time to apply to college in 1979, I again shunned economics. I wanted to specialize in something related to business. I applied and got accepted into the Bachelor of Commerce program at the University of Toronto. This confused my family. I can still hear my mother say proudly, "My son, the economist!" My maternal grandmother, Bobi Regina, whom I adored, would later brag to her friends that "my grandson is majoring in home economics," as if making soap were the same as drawing supply and demand curves.

Halfway through my first year, I learned that accounting was not my calling in life. Managerial accounting was fine; it was financial accounting where I struggled most. If you want to be an accountant, the most basic course is financial accounting. If memory serves correctly, I was failing miserably. For whatever reason, I couldn't balance out the T-accounts. I met with my professor, Gary Lee, who was great. In those days, the folks who taught accounting were lecturers who did this part time; they were full-time accountants on Bay Street. Gary toiled for Arthur Andersen, which is now, like Merrill Lynch and Gluskin Sheff, resting in peace. "Dave, your biggest shortfall is in those T-accounts," Gary told me. "I can't recall one exam where you got one of them right."

"So what do you recommend to students like me who can't balance the books?" I asked.

"Oh, I tell all of them what I'm about to tell you. Go into economics."

I dropped accounting and majored in economics. Sorry, Dad. It didn't cost me any lost time because you had to take Economics 101 as part of the commerce program and the course was far more rooted in reality than the high school version.

I'd got lucky my first year. In the summer of 1979, I spent the summer working as a volunteer on a kibbutz in northern Israel. Being far away with spotty mail service, I was late in sending in my class choices to the administration office. I had to spend my first week at university reapplying for my course load while my new friends were busy getting drunk during the fabled orientation week. All the popular classes were filled by the time I was reapplying, and all that was left for my first-semester course load were evening classes aimed at older students who were working during the day.

It turned out to be a blessing. Being in class with people in their thirties and forties who were seasoned and involved in their own businesses brought a certain degree of reality and practicality to economic theory. I learned as much from their questions and experiences as I did from the actual coursework. Also, my first economics lecturer was Bill Wolfson, who during the day was a practicing economist with the Ontario government. He was arguably the best educator I have ever met. His ability to distill and simplify complex topics—Giffen goods, marginal and average cost curves, monopolistic competition, elasticities, the backward supply curve of labor, etc.—was incredible. He was so good that my great friend, Jeff Trossman, stopped attending his class and joined me for Wolfson's lectures.

I knew early on that I'd found my true passion in economics. It blended so many subjects, from math to statistics to psychology to history. For a generalist like me, this was the perfect profession. As I like to tell people when asked about my background, "Economists are really accountants with personality." Even if we can't balance the books so well.

Switching paths was a blessing for me, and I'm not alone in that. My good pal, Jeff Trossman, thought he was going to be an economist forever, and nobody had his credentials: he not only won the gold medal in economics at the University of Toronto, but also received a PhD scholarship to MIT. He went to work for the Bank of Canada, and had he stayed there, I am positive he would have been governor. While I made my pivot in my early twenties, Jeff was closing in on thirty when he enrolled in law school. He became one of the top corporate tax lawyers on Bay Street.

Another great friend and mentor, Ken Bercuson, had a multifaceted career as an emerging market economics specialist at the International Monetary Fund, the head of a research department at a major Wall Street investment bank, an economist role on the bond and FX desk at Merrill Lynch, and he closed his incredible career as an advisor at a New York–based hedge fund. My dear brother, Mel, graduated with a doctorate in microbiology, spent many years as a college professor running labs, patenting an array of technologies aimed at curing oral health issues along that path (including the world's first bad-breath detector), and then, in his sixties, he was the founder of an online book publishing company. He is now an author of children's books.

There are many lessons here, especially for young people contemplating their futures. When older people advise you to "follow your passion," I would refine that to "let your passion follow you." Don't force things. Be sure to expose yourself and broaden your horizons. Don't get pigeonholed and if you do, as was the case with me, don't hesitate to try something new. Don't make assumptions about what you think you will want to do in the future. As Tom Hanks elegantly put it at the end of *Cast Away*: "Tomorrow the sun will rise. Who knows what the tide could bring?"

CHAPTER 3

Youthful Error

The summer of 1981 is one I'll never forget. I had just finished my second year at the University of Toronto, working toward my undergraduate degree in economics. Like most twenty-one-year-olds, I thought I knew everything.

I returned home for a summer job at a health food store, where I was responsible for inventory, working the cash register, and hauling bags of rice, flour, and coffee beans up and down three flights of stairs from the basement to the ground floor. In those four short weeks, I learned a lot—not just about running a store, but also about working for a real shyster. Every time I went to deposit my weekly paycheck, it bounced. Despite repeated promises of full payment, none were ever fulfilled. Realizing I was working for free, I decided I'd had enough.

My dad's best friend owned a prestigious grocery store in the city, and he convinced his pal to hire me for the rest of the summer as a stockboy, loading and unloading trucks. The watermelons were tricky. The owner wasn't just my dad's best friend; his entire family had been friends with my family for decades. I was happy to be working in a retail store again, learning how these businesses operate, even at the summer student level. Within weeks, I was promoted to the cellar to cut lettuce and other vegetables, and soon after that, I was moved to the main floor to create attractive displays of fruits and vegetables. I was treated well, except for the pranks my high school dropout coworkers played on me—like telling me

I had something in my eye after I unloaded a box of jalapeño peppers, or taking the ladder away when I was asked to hang a sign outside advertising bananas for fifty-nine cents a bunch.

Halfway through that summer of '81, I overheard some full-time workers discuss forming a union. I approached them and mentioned that I had just completed an industrial relations course at U of T, taught by John Crispo, a well-known and respected political economist in Canada. His was not only the most entertaining course I took during my five years at university, but the most informative. The entire course focused on labor-management relations, and we had guest speakers who were both CEOs and union representatives. I learned a great deal that year—perhaps too much.

When the workers at the store learned of my interest in helping them unionize and that I had some knowledge of the process, they asked me to be their consultant, a role I gladly accepted. They had already contacted the appropriate labor union for representation, so my role was simply to advise. Over several secret evening meetings at the home of a senior employee, attended by others eager to begin the certification process, the union representative soon arrived with a plan. I contributed my academic knowledge and opinions on the strategy, all gleaned from an undergraduate course on labor-management relations.

That summer, while having dinner at home, my dad mentioned that his friend, who ran the company, was facing a worker revolt and the possibility of unionization. I shrugged it off. However, for the next week, every evening my father brought up his friend's distress over the situation. I remained silent. Finally, my dad asked point-blank, "Dave, do you know anything about this union business?" Frozen and sweating, I lied and said, "I have no clue." For the following week, the topic resurfaced at every dinner. Each time, my dad would ask, "Dave, are you sure you know nothing about this union?" I continued to lie, becoming increasingly uncomfortable. Finally, my dad said, "If the workers unionize, my friend is going to close the entire business, fire everyone, and reopen with a new staff."

Well.

Suddenly, I felt pangs of guilt. I knew the man who ran this business well and sensed that his threats should be taken seriously. As I became more involved in the unionization drive, even indirectly, I felt like I was in over my head. After several raucous meetings with the union representatives, I realized they were probably even bigger jerks than the men managing the fruit and vegetable company. The pressure tactics the union reps used to get workers to sign the certification cards were, in a word, aggressive. Maybe sometimes it's better the devil you know than the devil you don't, but the more I saw these union bullies in action, the more I wanted to extricate myself from the situation entirely.

So, one beautiful summer Sunday afternoon, I went for a long walk with my mother, a wise owl. Her Yiddish name was actually Faigel, meaning bird. She gave me a real bird's-eye view of the entire situation. I told her what was really happening at this food and vegetable shop, about my indirect involvement, and how I had lied to Dad, right to his face. I remember that day as if it were yesterday.

My mother wasn't really upset with me, but was more sympathetic. She said I was half naïve and half ideological and reminded me that she was very sensitive to the labor union movement, having grown up in Winnipeg, where socialism was influential for many years. (Read about the great strike of 1919, and you'll know what I mean.) I was ideological, but who isn't at twenty-one? How could I have known back then how ridiculous it was to think I had everything figured out just because I took John Crispo's second-year course in industrial relations?

The big problem was lying to my dad. My mother told me, in no uncertain terms, that I was not to hide the lie from him any longer: "Come clean and tell your father the truth." This, too, remains fresh in my memory more than forty years later. As bad as it was admitting that I had surreptitiously worked behind the scenes to undermine his best friend's business, admitting that I'd lied about it for over a month was far worse. It hurt in a way that still brings a tear to my eye.

My father was furious. It was a painful double blow. His son had worked against his best friend, a friend who had given me a paid opportunity in his shop, unlike the unpaid work at the health food store. And his son had lied about it. We didn't speak for most of the rest of the summer.

During another walk we took, my mother said something that resonated with me then, and still does today. "Dave," she said, "your intentions were good, but all the lying to your father is completely unacceptable. You also have to consider the consequences of your actions. You're a temporary worker at the store; you'll be back in Toronto for your third year of economics in September. You won't bear any of the consequences of what's happening at the store, regardless of whether you were directly or indirectly involved. Other people, including the workers, whether they get unionized or not, will bear those consequences. If your dad's friend decides to close the shop, they will bear the consequences. If the certification process turns into a disaster, they will bear the consequences. But not you; you'll be back at school."

I continued to work at the store, doing my best to distance myself from the labor representatives and the unionization process. Still, I sensed that management knew of my involvement. My dad's friend, the owner, became quite cool toward me, and I hoped that whatever he knew wouldn't damage his long, close friendship with my father. My dad, meanwhile, continued the silent treatment. He was justifiably angry. It was one of the most painful periods of my life.

Although I successfully extricated myself from the unionization effort and stopped attending meetings after confessing to my father, it didn't matter. In mid-August, I received a letter from the Ontario Labour Relations

Board, summoning me to testify about the management practices that had triggered the certification process. I was instructed to appear at a specific date and time with two of the union representatives. We would be sitting across from my dad's best friend.

I seem to recall throwing up after reading the letter. Not only was I involved in this union business, and not only had I lied to my dad, but now I had to face his best friend, testify about employment standards violations, and likely ruin a friendship my dad valued immensely.

As fate would have it, I really did get sick. Within days of receiving the notice to appear before the tribunal that would determine the fate of the unionization drive, I developed a painful sore throat. I was beyond fatigued. My body broke out in rashes. Although my father still wasn't talking to me, he and my mother drove me to a clinic for a diagnosis. I had mononucleosis.

The physician told me I had to stay in bed for at least four weeks. I explained that I had to appear before a tribunal in the coming week, and the doctor said, "I will write you a note to excuse you from this endeavor because you are not to get out of bed, unless it's to go to the washroom." So, the doctor wrote the note, and I was absolved from having to testify against my dad's buddy about all the bad behavior at the company. It was like picking up a truly great Community Chest card in Monopoly: Skip the Labour Board hearings and go straight to GO. I didn't need to collect $200 to be completely elated by this turn of events.

As it turned out, the clowns and jackasses at the union never managed to get enough workers to sign the cards. The drive to unionize the company hit the proverbial wall, and my father's relationship with the owner of the company was saved. Best of all, Dad started talking to me again. I can't tell you how many times I apologized, even years later. My dad forgave me, but I realized that, of all the mistakes I made in this situation, the lying was the absolute worst. You can be excused for youthful exuberance and feeling, as a college student, that you can change the world. You can even be excused for aligning yourself with bad people (so long as you realize when to get out!). But again, not being truthful was the worst part of this and the greatest learning lesson.

The major takeaways? Honesty is always the best policy. Don't stick your nose where it doesn't belong. Listen to your mother. Try to be practical, not ideological. If you get sick, time it right.

CHAPTER 4

Economics, the House of Order

Later in my career, I began to appreciate economics not just in the financial and business world, but in society in general. Of course, there are Nobel laureates such as Harry Markowitz, who won the award for his work on modern portfolio theory; Robert Mundell, for his analysis of optimal currency areas; and Robert Merton and Myron Scholes, for valuing derivatives. However, many Nobel Prize winners, from Samuelson to Kuznets to Hicks to Arrow to Hayek to Tobin to Solow to Becker to Stiglitz to Akerlof to Kahneman, and even the libertarian Friedman, were economists whose research focused more on improving society than on making money.

Economics is both a social science and an art form, but at its core, it seeks to improve the world. That may have been what attracted me most to the profession. In my first microeconomics course, I learned that the intersection of supply and demand is "the bliss point," or, in more common terms, "the equilibrium." Where demand and supply cross, nobody benefits from moving up or down either curve.

The laws of supply and demand are basic tenets of economics, which makes sense because the word "economics" comes from the Greek words "eco" (order) and "nomous" (house). Together, they literally mean "house of order." Economics is about helping the house—euphemistically, the world—establish order and social stability, a tall task at the best of times.

I grew up in a family of educators. My mother was a kindergarten teacher, my dad taught part-time at the University of Ottawa, my sister Miriam was a well-recognized English teacher, my sister Rena was a public health nurse with a degree in education, and my brother Mel was a university professor for decades. What better way to contribute to society than to teach? While my experience in education was limited to being a teaching assistant in graduate school, I always found my profession to be a major contributor to improving the world.

Of course, economists are as heterogeneous as any other profession. Most doctors and lawyers have their own specialties, and the same is true in economics. Some work in academia, some at central banks, some as civil servants, and some at think tanks. And, of course, some work in the business world and financial markets. That's the route I took, simply because I enjoy the fast pace.

At the intersection of supply and demand, you can't improve someone's situation without worsening someone else's. In my industry, that intersection is where the markets clear, where everything is in balance. So, in my sphere, everyone always wants to know the answer to one singular question: "Where is the price going?" That includes the price of everything: food, oil, gold, industrial commodities, real estate, bonds, stocks—you name it. I discovered the power of understanding the shape of demand and supply curves and forecasting how these lines will shift in the future. This toolkit helps generate what everyone wants to know: the future price of anything. Who doesn't want to know where the price is going?

Of course, economists bear the responsibility of ensuring these curves are drawn accurately and their predicted movements, up or down, are correct. Over my four-decade career, I have had my share of failures and successes. When I have missed the mark, it has generally been from underestimating the demand curve—supply curves tend to be easier to draw and predict. This was especially true when it came to the rampant cycles of asset inflation we have witnessed over the past several decades. My conservative mindset led me to underestimate the demand curve.

To some extent, that obscures the bigger point: don't provide your client with just one set of curves. In the forecasting business, your conclusions hinge on the assumptions you make. Tweak the assumptions even slightly, and the conclusions (being the price) can be materially altered. It behooves the economist to always couple their base-case forecast with a range of possible outcomes.

Helping people in my business means ruling nothing out and providing various scenarios with probabilities attached. This is what makes economists so valuable, despite the ridicule they typically face on trading floors. We have tools to help decision-makers plan for the future. There is a deep, symbiotic relationship between economists and strategists. They need each other. The strategist leans heavily on the economist because the strategist is required to constantly ascertain what is being priced into the markets and sectors they cover. Economists are paid to forecast that price. This is why every investment bank and financial institution has an economics department.

It's a profession that never goes out of style.

CHAPTER 5

The Weed and Grass Summer

Students who don't take summer jobs miss out on a lot. During the summer of 1982, between my third and fourth year at the University of Toronto, I worked at a family-run firm called Metro Weed Control, spraying weeds.

Every day, as long as it wasn't raining, I received a list of a dozen houses. With my spraying apparatus, I walked up and down the front and back yards in the blazing heat. That was the entire job. My uniform consisted of a pair of shorts, a grubby T-shirt, and a baseball cap, likely because a real uniform would have reeked. To be honest, I stank anyway. I'd return to my roommates, and they'd shout, 'Rosie, straight to the shower!' Just thinking of the smell sends shivers down my spine. The chemicals definitely weren't the safest, and to this day, I wonder why I don't have six toes on my right foot.

Halfway through the season, a salesperson left, and the owner asked the sprayers if anyone wanted to step into a sales role. I shot my hands up, shouting, "Me! Me! Me!" Now, instead of spraying weeds, I went door-to-door selling spring and fall spray and fertilizer. I started by putting flyers in mailboxes and then progressed to knocking on doors. This was before the Internet. I couldn't look anyone up or Google "sales techniques." I had to develop my own style. I earned a commission on every sale, which was a great incentive, and soon enough, I became their top salesperson.

My strategy was to explain that I was a summer student at the University of Toronto, a starving student just trying to get by. It's a fine art to suggest someone needs weed control without offending them or implying their lawn is worse than their neighbors' lawns. Did doors get slammed in my face? Absolutely. It's like baseball—you have to strike out a lot to score.

My most memorable sale happened right after Italy won the World Cup. I saw an older gentleman on his knees beside his house, picking dandelions by hand. I said to him, "This is not something a man of your age should be doing." I realize now he wasn't that old, probably my age today, so no wonder he said,

"No, no, no. I do things on my own."

I didn't know what to say, so I said, "Viva Italia!"

He said, "You're Italian? Come into my house!"

I'm not Italian, but I had recently watched *The Godfather*. Before I knew it, we were drinking homemade red wine at his kitchen table. He bought about three years' worth of spray and fertilizer—breaking every record. The only problem was that I was too drunk to drive and had to walk an hour and a half back home.

That summer, at twenty-two years old, I realized for the first time that I had a gift for communicating and convincing someone to do something they might not otherwise do. When you're selling, you're really selling yourself, whether you're representing fertilizer or research. Of course, some may say they're one and the same.

CHAPTER 6

A Useful Step Backward

I was hired as a housing policy economist straight out of grad school, and spent three years with Canada Mortgage and Housing Corporation (CMHC) in Ottawa. It was an interesting time because Brian Mulroney had just become prime minister after the Conservatives had been out of power for decades (aside from the brief Joe Clark government in 1979–1980). The Conservatives were busy evaluating every Liberal program, many of which had been around since 1954, and housing was a particular area of focus. I had plenty to do.

My experience at CMHC taught me a great deal about cost-benefit analysis, but also about government bureaucracy, which was of less interest. Even though I was steadily promoted and learning a lot, I longed to move from Ottawa to Toronto. I knew nothing about Bay Street, but I felt I'd fit in best there; call it intuition. I applied to the economics departments at all the big banks.

The Bank of Nova Scotia was my only offer: a junior economist position at $27,500 a year. In Ottawa, where the cost of living was lower, I was a senior policy analyst at CMHC earning $32,000. When I pointed out the discrepancy between their offer and my current salary and title, the Scotia folks said, "David, 'junior' in Toronto is what 'senior' is in Ottawa, and we can't budge on salary." I was about to turn down the offer until my dad gave me some advice: "Dave, sometimes in life, you have to take a step back to take two steps forward. Before you turn them down, look at the bigger picture. Where will you be if you stay in government five or ten years from now, and where do you think you'll be if you take this offer?"

That was Dad. I took the job. Day one was Black Monday, October 19, 1987. I still remember the panicked traders on the trading floor. I could have gotten a return ticket to my cushy job in Ottawa, and I would have taken it in a heartbeat.

As mentioned earlier, I spent the entire day, my first as a bona fide street economist, shadowing Bill Mackness, Warren Jestin, and Aron Gampel. At each meeting, I stood at the back of the room, figuratively changing my underwear every hour. My three bosses presented charts to the senior brass arguing that the crash was a liquidity event, not a fundamental one. They said that the Federal Reserve and the Bank of Canada would infuse tremendous amounts of liquidity into the financial system, and it would all be over in a week; the bank should be buying the market. I remember thinking, "Holy smoke, economists who actually call the market. These guys are fearless." I began to feel that "cool economist" wasn't an oxymoron—you could be cool and be an economist at the same time. Warren Jestin and Aron Gampel had ice in their veins.

I learned on day one that to be an effective market economist, you can't just analyze GDP. You have to attach market calls to your forecasts. You have to take all the economic data points and connect them to a cogent, coherent investment strategy. In the end, all everyone wants to know is how they can make or save money.

Senior management at the bank didn't buy into the view of Bill, Warren, and Aron. Like most people at the time, the brass thought the world was ending. In the days after the crash, it cut half of the bank's research budget, including economics research. Within weeks, half of the economics department was let go. I remember Aron telling me one morning to stay in my office all day and not come out. I was so freaked out that I might have hidden under my desk. That evening, there was a farewell party for those who were packaged out, some of whom had been at the bank for twenty-five years. Unfortunately for them, layoff decisions were based on survival of the fittest, not seniority.

Everyone was hugging and crying. As the new kid on the block, I remember telling myself that I was never going to let that happen to me. Or, if it did, my boss and my boss's boss would be falling on their swords at the same time if they ever had to let me go.

For the next six months, I was supposed to be mentored by one of the senior economists. I didn't know my ass from my elbow. Nothing I had learned in graduate school in economics or at CMHC was going to help me on Bay Street. With all the layoffs, the mentoring plan fell by the wayside in favor of on-the-job training. I did have a tutor in the economics department, but she left for a promotion at Royal Bank of Canada a few weeks after I started, and I was told to pick up the slack. It was sink or swim in a pool of sharks with no life preserver.

The "slack" included presenting at the morning meetings to the treasury group, which was intimidating to say the least. I had all these writing assignments and no training. For weeks, draft after draft came back from Warren and Aron totally rewritten and covered in red Xs. I thought I was going to be fired. But I took hold of myself and, after a good cry, told my pals not to bug me to go out to the pubs.

I went into the office on a Saturday and photocopied everything—I mean everything—that Warren and Aron had produced for the prior three years. This was before the Internet. I stood at the photocopier all day and took home six boxes of their published work. I spent the next three weeks reading and rereading, telling myself, "You are going to get in their heads and figure out what makes them tick."

A week or two later, a report I wrote was returned to my desk unblemished. I went to Aron's office. He wasn't there. I went to Warren's office. Warren, who was soon to become the chief economist, was standing at his door. "Warren," I said, "I gave this piece to you and Aron to review, and it was sitting on my desk without a mark. Did you have a look at it?" Warren tried hard not to smirk, but he did, and said, "Dave, you finally get it." I went out on such a bender that night that I showed up to work the next morning wearing two different shoes.

Not long after I started Rosenberg Research in early 2020, a client's son, who had just begun working in capital markets at the Bank of Nova Scotia, called to ask me about the "secret to success." My initial reply was a bit glib: I told him to maintain a healthy level of paranoia. At his request, I elaborated, sharing the story about my first days at the bank. I explained the value of shadowing, of seeking out mentors, rather than assuming they will magically appear. I told him about my fear of getting fired, and how nothing can replace experience, and that we're never too old to learn. I told him that the Bank of Nova Scotia gets tons of CVs from candidates with high IQs, but IQ is a commodity—it can be taught.

Emotional intelligence, or EQ, is different. It's about character, integrity, responsibility, work ethic, courage, ownership of mistakes, team-playing, and trust. Those are qualities you cannot teach, and it's your EQ that will make the difference in your ability to make clear decisions, your relationships with colleagues and clients, and, ultimately, your success.

"It must be good for you not to have a boss anymore," the kids said.

"Actually," I replied, "I have more than one boss. I have over 4,000 of them, otherwise known as my clients, and the reality is that you never stop having a boss, even when you think you don't have one."

CHAPTER 7

Punch Above Your Job Description

I was recently interviewing candidates for junior positions here at the firm, and the question of how to achieve success in one's commercial or business life arose, as it tends to do with those entering the workforce for the first time. The answer is quite simple: don't settle for meeting the minimum job requirements. Aim higher, because that's the only way to prove to your employer that you're ready for new responsibilities and the better compensation that comes with them. It's like playing chess: think two or three moves ahead.

I can only draw on my own experiences, and two from my time as a young economist resonate most.

The first involved my boss, Aron Gampel, who was number two in the Scotiabank economics department. Not long after I was hired, I was tasked with splitting the morning meetings with Aron on the sales and trading desk. Coming from my comfortable job as a housing economist in Ottawa, my knowledge of financial markets was limited, at best. I was instructed to learn quickly. Sink or swim, in other words. It was daunting.

The masters of the universe on the trading floor initially took it easy on me because they felt sorry for me. When they started hurling insults, I knew I must be doing a decent job—the traders and sales folks no longer felt they needed to hold back. After about three months of facing this typically hostile crowd every morning, I began to get comfortable. I figured out that these people, the money makers at the bank, were the ones who took the risk and had their necks on the line. They were relying on me. I began to appreciate my overwhelming responsibility to be on the right side of the call. Also, that they were my clients. And so, I treated them like clients, meaning I would bleed for them, doing whatever it took to give them an edge over their competitors on Bay Street.

My day would go like this. I'd arrive at 6:30 in the morning. I had noticed early on that Aron got to the office at 7:00 a.m. sharp, and I wanted to be there when he arrived. It's always best to show up at work before your boss. Aron and I would usually head to the trading floor around 7:30 a.m., split up for the next hour, and then meet at the local coffee shop before returning to the office to write the "wire," a daily market commentary that typically went out by 10:00 a.m. For the first few years, Aron would basically dictate the note to me, and then I would sit behind our administrative assistant (they were still called secretaries then) to dictate my scrubbed notes to her, like an assembly line. Seeing "Gampel/Rosenberg" at the top right of the one-pager gave me a charge. Unlike the federal government bureaucracy where I had worked for the previous three years, people were actually reading this stuff.

After I started figuring things out, I began to get adept at the rudimentary Telerate machine, and I also started developing some contacts on the London trading desk, where there was a five-hour time difference. That gave me a wealth of information about what had been happening around the world. News moved very slowly in the mid- to late 1980s. Early every morning, I jotted down notes and then went straight to the newspapers for more. I started printing five or six (never more) bullet points in large font on a single page, titled "Daily Highlights." These were quick snippets of what had happened overnight, how that was affecting North American markets, and what the likely flashpoints would be that day, all to help the sales force and traders prepare for the next eight hours. I photocopied them and handed them out at my meetings.

After the first few days of doing this (and it won me friends on the trading floor), I could see it was a home run. I hadn't yet told Aron what I was up to, but after seeing the initial positive response to the prototype, I showed one to him before one of our early morning treks to the trading room. He looked at it and asked, "Did you make any copies for me?" I said, "Well, I didn't want to assume that you would like it enough to hand it out at your meetings." The next day, I made sure to give him a copy of these bullets before we left our office for the morning meetings. I poked my head out of my office and saw him making copies at the Xerox. Yes!

The second experience occurred about a year into the job. I was an intermediate-level economist, and Warren Jestin was the chief economist. Every Monday at 1:00 p.m., he held a regular meeting called the Liability Meeting with the eight most senior people at the bank, including the CEO, Cedric Ritchie, and the president, Gordon Bell (both intimidating individuals, to put it mildly). During my first year at the bank, Warren would come to my office about two hours before the Liability Meeting with questions about the data. Not my opinions—he always had queries about the data. At one point, I had a eureka moment. I figured out how to fit all the data he needed for the meeting onto one page, and also how to automate the process.

I came into the office for three weekends and managed to do it. The result looked like the play cards that NFL coaches use on the sidelines, though it wasn't color-coded, although I did manage to shade some regions of the page. Nor was it laminated. It had everything: the broad trends in the economic numbers, financial market data, and the credit aggregates, all on one page.

Once I finished this self-imposed task, I knocked on Warren's door the following Monday around 10:00 a.m. "Warren, can I talk to you for a few minutes?"

I sheepishly said, "I want to show you something."

"Sure, come in."

I handed him the page.

"What's this?"

I explained that I'd noticed he had the same or similar data questions before every Liability Meeting, so I thought I would prepare a one-pager for him.

Silence.

"When did you find time to do this?"

"Oh, I came into the office over the past three weekends."

"But why?"

"Well, I consider it a core part of my job to make your job easier."

Silence again.

With some trepidation, I asked, "Warren, do you like it?"

He smirked (generally a good sign) and responded, "Can you slide in M2 and M3 at the bottom?"

Six months later, I was promoted to senior economist.

This was solely because I went above and beyond my job description, sacrificed three weekends, took initiative, and showed my boss that I had his back.

CHAPTER 8

The Chief Economist's Speech

If you've never seen the movie *The King's Speech*, I highly recommend it. It won four Academy Awards, including Best Picture, fifteen years ago. In essence, it's about how King George VI coped with a stammer and, through intense therapy and learning, delivered the most important speech of his life when Britain declared war on Germany in 1939.

What does this have to do with me? Not much, but it resonates with me because I had a similar problem early in my career. Not a stutter, but an inability to deliver a speech that could excite an audience—or even keep their attention for five minutes.

Just before the holidays in 1989, I gave my very first speech. I was still an intermediate economist at the Bank of Nova Scotia and a rather inexperienced twenty-nine-year-old. Warren Jestin was asked to give a speech for some association, I believe it was the Kiwanis Club. The event was in Brampton, Ontario, about thirty miles northwest of Toronto, at the Marriott, if memory serves. It was the club's annual Christmas party. There was some connection between the association and the Bank of Nova Scotia, but Warren didn't want to do the speech. In mid-December, he came to me and said, "Dave, you're about to give your first speech," and handed it off.

My initial trepidation turned to excitement. I spent days writing and rewriting my speech.

There were about 200 people in the ballroom, with a partition at the back (more on that later). I was at the head table, heart pounding, barely touching my meal. Before long, I was introduced by the MC. I headed to the podium, pulled my reams of paper from my pocket, and placed my handwritten notes on the lectern, and began:

> Good evening, ladies and gentlemen. It is with tremendous honor that I deliver to you this evening the global economic outlook for 1990 as we see it at the Bank of Nova Scotia's economics department.
>
> We are of the view that in the aftermath of the rapid tightening in monetary policy this past year by the Bank of Canada, real GDP growth will moderate to 2.25 percent in 1990 from 3.25 percent in 1989. This slowdown will be reinforced by the complications surrounding the implementation of the US–Canada free trade agreement and, of course the distortions which will most assuredly create much economic volatility from the looming Goods and Services Tax.
>
> We are of the view that consumer spending will slow to 2.15 percent from 3.35 percent these past twelve months, as the household sector responds to the lagged impacts of the rise in interest rates and the rise in the unemployment rate.
>
> The housing market will not be unaffected. Indeed, the employment situation will be rather dire and this will very likely weigh on the residential real estate sector. We cannot be sure how the business sector will be responding but we are seeing many, many signs of reduced capital spending intentions and have noticed a particularly disappointing trend in primary metals, fabricated metals, pipeline equipment, cement and concrete, transistors, heavy trucking, railroad track, electrical and electronic products, corrugated boxes, and the like.

You can see where this is going. I droned on and on, reading every detailed, boring word of my speech. It was totally monotonous and it went on forever:

> Now allow me to describe the outlook for inflation, the way we see it at the Bank of Nova Scotia's economics department. But before I get into the most recent developments on labour union contracts, let me first describe what we are seeing in terms of the behavior of the monetary and credit aggregates . . .

I could have sworn I heard someone whisper, "Please don't." I continued. A half-hour in, and I was only one-third of the way through my notes. I could see some fidgeting, but I continued. Another fifteen minutes, and I was halfway through. I was barely through the US view and still had Asia and Europe to go!

Then someone at the back of the ballroom opened the partition door. Behind it was a brightly lit casino with blackjack, roulette, and craps tables. Undeterred, I continued my monologue. A few minutes later, I noticed a couple of people sneak to the casino, then a few more, then more after that. Soon half the room had left the tables. I was almost an hour into my spiel, and I was now speed-reading aloud. It was painful. If you've seen *Broadcast News*, think of the scene when Albert Brooks is a news anchor for the first time and soils his shirt. Well, I soiled a lot more than that. Sweat poured off me as if I were running a marathon. But I kept plugging along.

Soon, after seventy-five minutes of pure hell for the Kiwanis folks—I was ruining their Christmas party!—three-quarters of the audience were at the casino. By the time I finally closed with my view of the Japanese stock market (I hope I said it was at an all-time peak, never to be seen again, but I truly don't remember), about fifteen polite souls remained. "That concludes my remarks," I said. "Thank you very much and happy holidays." I don't think I ever received such wild applause in my entire professional life.

I had some pretty bad thoughts on the way home, but I won't go there. Visions of Jimmy Stewart in *It's a Wonderful Life* swirled in my head.

I knew I blew it. I mean, it was so bad I almost passed out on stage. I swore I would never again read a speech or drone on for ninety minutes again. But what happened next was interesting.

A week later, Warren came to my office and said, "Dave, I'm giving a breakfast speech up the street at the Four Seasons. Care to join me?" I think I was at the elevator before he finished.

Warren told me to stand at the back of the room and take mental notes. When he went to the stage, he started with a funny joke, and his speech was informative and entertaining. The entire crowd was engaged. And he had no notes! His eyes never wandered from the crowd. Warren was also his usual sardonic and sarcastic self, and people loved it. He included anecdotes to keep things interesting. His style resonated. I also noticed how tight his message was at the outset: "These are the three major themes." Bing, bang, boom! "This is why they are relevant for shaping what's to come for the economy and the markets. Here's what sets this view apart from the consensus." Eureka! I got it right away.

That experience never left me. Not only did nobody leave the room when Warren spoke—he kept it to thirty minutes—but he got a standing ovation. On the walk back to the office, I kept saying to myself: "I want to be him!"

As I said, I didn't have a stutter like the King. I just had to learn, and it took years to develop a technique to keep a crowd engaged. I had other tutors and mentors along the way. Don Coxe was a huge inspiration and will always be the best in the business, in my opinion. Niall Ferguson and Paul McCulley are riveting speakers I've watched closely. To this day, I try to pick up valuable tips from the best. The key is not to copy their style. That is something we each own because it's part of our personality and individuality. But you can learn from watching them and make it work for you.

When people ask me what it takes to give a great speech, I think back to that initial bomb thirty-seven years ago and give them the benefit of my mistakes: drop the notes, talk clearly and with authority, make constant eye contact, and have a differentiated and unique story with a relevant conclusion for the audience. And, if you can, leave them laughing at your jokes, not your performance.

CHAPTER 9

Keep Your Friends Close, and Your Calendar Closer

Two incidents stick in my mind from my time as senior economist at BMO Nesbitt Burns. The first was the near-demise of our country during the Quebec vote on sovereignty-association on October 30, 1995. The "non" option, against breaking up Canada, won by a hair.

Nobody in my department or on the trading desk went home that night. We had prepared two reports to send out, one on the implications of a "oui" vote for separation, and another on a "non" vote. The final result wasn't announced until the wee hours of the morning. The Canadian dollar had no bid through the entire night. I admit there was a ton of fear about what a Quebec split would mean; we are talking about more than 20 percent of the country's GDP and population becoming its own sovereign nation (albeit with a Canadian passport and the Canadian dollar, or so the hoodwink campaign by the separatists had it).

I wrote our piece on what would happen to the economy, currency, interest rates, and markets had Quebec voted to split. My pal and colleague, Doug Porter, now chief economist at the bank, had the pleasure of being chosen to write the report on what would happen if Quebec chose to stay. Sherry Cooper knew that if anyone was adept at writing a horror story, it was yours truly.

When it came time to press the button, Doug's report was published, not mine. If you are Canadian, you definitely do not want to know what my conclusions were. Thankfully, all for nothing.

* * *

The other incident that stands out was a lunch in the summer of 1998.

The Bank of Canada had established a Toronto office and appointed a senior official to serve as a liaison with Bay Street. In the late 1990s, the second person to hold this position was someone I knew. We had many economist friends in common, and over time, we became friends. Let's call this person "F," as warm and engaging an individual as you could ever hope to meet.

We would periodically have lunch, usually sushi, and discuss the economy, markets, and life in general. Our conversations never crossed any ethical lines, and F never divulged any confidential information about the bank's internal deliberations or decisions. F's role was primarily to facilitate effective communication between the bank and the market, and I could contribute (although I was certainly not F's only contact on Bay Street) by providing insights into the prevailing economic sentiment and outlining my own perspectives.

When we had lunch in the summer of 1998, the Canadian dollar was under intense downward pressure due to considerable market volatility. The situation became so destabilizing that the Bank of Canada aggressively raised interest rates to support the currency. With a policy meeting approaching, F and I intentionally avoided discussing the economy or the markets. At no point did F indicate the bank's likely course of action. Not a word about it. Besides, F wasn't privy to that information. We were simply two friends catching up on our personal lives.

At BMO Nesbitt Burns, where I was working at the time, there was considerable debate within the economics department about the Bank of Canada's next move. I've always adhered to the Mosaic Theory of financial and economic research, incorporating information from all publicly available sources to formulate my forecasts. Based on my own analysis, I independently concluded that the Bank of Canada would likely hold steady at the upcoming meeting. However, I was also aware that the BMO Nesbitt Burns trading desk was positioned for another significant interest rate hike, creating a high risk

of being offside. I had already shared my assessment with my colleagues in the economics department, convincing them of the high likelihood of a "no-move" decision.

Later that afternoon, following my lunch with F, I made my usual rounds on the trading floor, discussing my views with the sales and trading desks across the money market, bond, and equity teams. I reiterated my opinion that the Bank of Canada would hold its fire. The head of the money market team was skeptical and questioned my view extensively.

A few months later, I had another lunch with F. This time, it was a frosty affair. Halfway through the meal, I finally asked, "F, what's going on?"

"Tell me you have no idea."

"What are you talking about?"

"Dave, you very nearly got me fired!"

I was stunned. Apparently, an individual ("R") on the BMO desk had called my assistant, without my permission, to inquire about my schedule and specifically asked if I had met with anyone from the government recently. Instead of dismissing the inquiry, she revealed that I had just had lunch with F, who was well-known and respected on Bay Street. R then shifted their trading position and, to cover the trade, contacted counterparties on Bay Street, falsely claiming I had received inside information about the Bank of Canada's next move and that I had lunch with F. I kid you not.

Can you imagine calling my assistant to find out who I was lunching with and then, to justify a trade, spreading rumors about insider information? I was shocked. F explained that the information had reached the Bank of Canada's leadership, triggering an investigation. Thankfully, F was exonerated, having done nothing wrong. However, the entire episode weighed heavily on me for a long time. F told me this would be our last lunch, leaving me utterly dejected. I felt terrible about what had happened and about my role in this unfortunate situation.

Years later, while recounting this story to some younger staff members in my office at another firm, a very senior person on the investment team ("X") was present. X posed a "what if" question, asking what I would have done if F had actually provided me with privileged information. X was astonished when I replied that I would have sought advice from the legal or compliance department and that I would never have considered sharing non-public information. X persisted, badgering me in front of the staff. He asked if I had ever obtained confidential information and if there were any circumstances under which I would "help the firm make money" by divulging what I knew. I again replied "no."

"You mean to tell me that if you received information, even improperly, you would not share it with me so I can turn a profit for the company we both work for?"

"No, not under any circumstances."

X concluded by saying, "Rosenberg, if I could fire you right now, I would pull the trigger."

As it turned out, it didn't matter, because I resigned shortly thereafter.

This story has haunted me for the past quarter-century. It was a painful experience, but it taught me a valuable lesson: avoid trading floors after lunching with anyone from a central bank, and ensure your assistant knows what information to keep private. Better yet, as an analyst, keep your opinions in print form, because loose lips can sink friendships.

Fortunately, the story has a happy ending. Shortly after my last lunch with F, I had left for New York and lost touch with many people in Canada. Recently, I found F online and reached out. We hadn't spoken in years, but quickly caught up over the phone. During our conversation, I reminded F of what had happened and apologized again. Remarkably, F barely remembered the incident and considered it a "non-event." We had a wonderful, warm conversation, just like in the old days. F didn't hate me after all! We recently went back out for sushi and wine, rekindling our friendship.

CHAPTER 10

The Business Traveler's Survival Guide

In 1996, the BMO/Nesbitt Burns bond desk in London asked me to go on a European marketing trip to meet with institutional clients. Paul Petrashko, a top salesperson on the fixed-income side and a fun, high-character traveling companion, led the trip.

It was a week-long journey through Europe, starting in Vienna, a city I had never visited. I had a layover in Amsterdam and arrived in Vienna on a Sunday—my first mistake, since everything was closed. The bond team from London had arrived the day before, a wiser decision. I stood at the carousel in the Vienna airport, waiting for my luggage after clearing immigration. Everyone else had collected their bags, but I continued to wait. And wait. And wait. For an hour, I watched the same round, pale-blue valise circle the carousel (it wasn't mine), and I had the sinking feeling that my suitcase hadn't made it on this leg of the journey. The dangers of connecting flights.

I was wearing jeans and a Montreal Canadiens jersey and ratty running shoes. I had no carry-on. My suit, shirts, ties, and dress shoes were all packed neatly in my suitcase, which was clearly somewhere else. And I had a client breakfast presentation at the hotel the next morning at 10:00 a.m. The best thing about European marketing trips is that, unlike in America, where these presentations start at 7:30 a.m., the Europeans take it slow, smell the coffee first, and get started at a much more reasonable hour.

At the airport, I went to the help desk and was told that my bag was still in Amsterdam and that KLM would fly it in later that day. It was early afternoon, and there were two more KLM flights arriving in Vienna. Arrangements were made, unnecessarily as it turned out, to deliver my suitcase to my hotel. I felt better, but not for long.

When I arrived at the hotel, I told my bond sales partners about my luggage mishap and said that I wanted to stay near the hotel phone in case there was news about my suitcase—remember, this was before cell phones. Paul kept telling me not to worry, which was somewhat soothing. Late in the afternoon, I called the airport, knowing that the next flight from Amsterdam had arrived. After what felt like hours on hold, an airport employee told me my suitcase was not on the flight. I wanted to ask Paul if I could begin worrying now.

There was only one flight left that day from Amsterdam to Vienna, arriving at 10:00 p.m. I planned to stay by the phone in my hotel room, but Paul convinced me to join him and his team for dinner, constantly telling me to relax. It turned out to be more drinks than dinner. Paul took us to a Russian vodka bar he frequented on his Vienna trips—bond sales folks at major banks often moonlighted as social alcoholics. They plied me with vodka and trout caviar (not beluga—these were bond guys, not equity guys). They succeeded in getting me drunk. My mental anguish about my suitcase lessened with each shot of vodka. I was still hoping my bag would arrive in time for my slideshow the next morning. At least Paul had the slides.

At 10:00 p.m., I used the bar's phone to call the airport. And, what do you know? No bag. No one at the airport or KLM knew where it was. I was beyond distressed. Paul and his team's solution was to give me more alcohol. I told Paul that my boss, Sherry Cooper, would surely chew me out, if not fire me, for giving my presentations in old jeans and a smelly hockey sweater. Paul, ever the optimist, said the clients would understand

and find it humorous. Not to worry! So, we drank more. I figured it was the only way to forget the dismal situation.

I woke up early Monday morning, realizing I was traveling throughout Europe all week—a city a day: Vienna, Brussels, Milan, Frankfurt, Paris, and finally London. And I had no business attire! I went to Paul's room around 7:30 a.m. and knocked. Of course, he was asleep. We were both materially hung over, but I didn't care. He groggily opened the door, and I said, "Guess what? I'm worried, and you and I are going shopping!" Paul spoke fluent German and knew Vienna inside out. Luckily, it was a ten-minute walk from the hotel to the shopping district.

I don't exactly fit off the rack, and I didn't back in the mid-1990s either, but we did our best. We found a clothing store that had my size (sort of), and I bought a blazer, two pairs of slacks, two ties, three dress shirts, and a pair of shiny black shoes. All the while, Paul played interpreter and fashion consultant. I went to the counter to pay, and the bill came to something like $3,000, which back then meant something. I must have looked shocked as I pulled out my credit card because Paul whispered, "Rosie, you aren't at Yorkdale shopping mall. You're in one of the most expensive shopping areas in Europe." Okay, I got it. Plus, I had no choice (pure price inelasticity on my part). It was already 8:30 in the morning, and I was to be on stage in ninety minutes.

All that was left was undergarments and socks. We found a department store. Paul told the sales lady I needed underwear, and her face turned white. I told Paul to explain that I was, in fact, wearing a pair (two days old, mind you). After buying some underwear and socks, plus a toothbrush, toothpaste, deodorant, and a comb, I was good to go. My blazer was an inch too long, and the slacks were a tad tight, but I didn't care. I'd get everything tailored when I got home.

As it turned out, buying multiples of everything was a stroke of genius. KLM kept calling to tell me my bag had arrived, but it always arrived in the prior city I had been in. The bag followed me around Europe all week, perpetually a day behind. It finally made its way to Toronto a week after I got home.

When I wore my new clothes to the office on Bay Street, everyone, including Sherry, would come up to me and say, "Nice threads, Rosenberg!" I would think to myself, "If you only knew." On my brother Mel's advice, I wrote a letter to KLM detailing my experience, and the airline asked me to send them the bills for the flashy apparel—socks and underwear included. It reimbursed me in full. It even sent me some airline lounge vouchers for my next stopover.

Had I known how it would all shake out, I would have closed that Russian bar with my BMO sales pals that first night. I have given some of my best presentations completely hungover, if not with some alcohol still in my system. But, to be honest, what I really would have done, and have done ever since, is take what I need in my carry-on on the plane.

CHAPTER 11

I Become a Media Outlet

A human resources guru once told me that almost everyone's professional success can be attributed to one inflection point, a particular event that often lasts no more than a few minutes. That definitely happened to me at the genesis of what would eventually become my daily bulletin.

In October 1998, while working at BMO Nesbitt Burns, I attended our annual client gala at the Royal Ontario Museum in Toronto. It was an important evening, featuring the legendary chef Jamie Kennedy, hundreds of the firm's top institutional clients, and a feature debate between chief economist Sherry Cooper, my boss, and the chief strategist at Harris Investment Management, Don Coxe, who became a dear friend and mentor to me. These annual Sherry-Don debates were always lively and entertaining.

Afterward, I was at the bar ordering a scotch when a man named Bill Downe approached me. "I've been waiting for a chance to meet you," he said. I almost choked on my single malt. Bill was a senior executive at the investment bank, recently promoted from a senior role south of the border to head the entire treasury operation out of the Toronto headquarters. What could he possibly want to talk to me about?

In those years, I presented at most of the treasury group's morning meetings, covering stocks, bonds, FX—you name it. I spent countless hours on the trading floor. As senior economist, I was responsible for the financial markets outlook, while my colleague and good friend Doug

Porter (now the chief economist at the Bank of Montreal) was primarily responsible for forecasting macroeconomic trends. And now, one of the most powerful people at BMO—he would become CEO of the entire bank from 2007 to 2017—was seeking me out. I was nervous.

"I've been attending your morning meetings since I arrived in Toronto."

"Uh oh," I thought.

He must have seen the worried look on my face because he quickly added, "Oh, don't get me wrong. Everyone loves your meetings. But you talk way too fast. The traders and salespeople can't keep up, and it becomes a classic case of broken telephone: 'What did Rosie say again?'"

Then came the key point. "I want you to put your morning meetings down on paper. In fact, I want it to become your own report—give it a catchy name—and we'll market the hell out of it."

I was reluctant at first. It meant extra work, extra pressure, and tangible evidence of incorrect calls. Plus, Sherry would likely be hesitant to add to my workload. But Bill wouldn't take no for an answer.

That month, my daily report was born. The title wasn't exactly "catchy"—it was called A.M. Notes. But it took off like a rocket ship. Before long, I really enjoyed writing it, even though it meant sacrificing an hour or two of sleep. Putting my observations in writing forced me to be more disciplined and confident, because there was no turning back after I hit "send." The Internet was still in its infancy, and A.M. Notes was a pioneer, launched long before economic and financial dailies became commonplace.

The daily was distributed throughout the bank and re-sent to clients—institutional, retail, and the media alike. Suddenly, I was being quoted in the morning papers (not unhappily, I should say—in the prima donna economics industry, a bit of notoriety is never unwelcome) and being asked by the equity and fixed income sales teams to meet with their institutional clients. In the months that followed, I met every important portfolio manager and CIO on Bay Street. Within a year, I began to be ranked in the

Brendan Wood survey of Canadian economists in the financial industry. The rankings were made sweeter still because I was the only "senior" economist ranked alongside the "chief" economists on Bay Street.

A.M. Notes became so popular that it was the primary reason Merrill Lynch Canada hired me away from BMO to be its Toronto-based chief economist and strategist in early 2000. The daily, which would undergo several name changes over the years, enjoyed an even broader distribution with the powerful Merrill sales force.

CHAPTER 12

The Accidental Tourist

Over my four decades in the financial industry, I had the pleasure of visiting many places around the world. Although, "visiting" might be a better word than "seeing," as these trips were almost always strictly business with little time for leisure. One exception was a trip to Europe with the same sales crew out of London, when I was with BMO Nesbitt Burns. It was another grueling journey: five cities in six days.

We finished in Rome, where it was just me and my pal, Paul Petrashko. On that last full day, several meetings were canceled, and all I had to do was a breakfast presentation at the hotel. It ended at 10:00 a.m., and Paul told me he was taking the next plane back to London. My flight back to Toronto wasn't until the next day. So, I ran to my room, changed into jeans and a polo shirt, grabbed a map from the concierge, and spent the entire day walking. I saw the Spanish Steps, the Trevi Fountain, the Colosseum, St. Peter's Basilica, and the Piazza Navona, squeezing three days of touring into one!

I returned to the hotel in the late afternoon, showered, changed, and asked the concierge to recommend a good restaurant within walking distance. I found a wonderful trattoria, ordered a huge plate of spaghetti and meatballs, and drank an entire bottle of Brunello. Afterward, I walked back to the Trevi Fountain to see it lit up at night, found a nice coffee shop, sat outside, and ordered a double espresso, a double anisette, and a double gelato (go big or go home). As I gazed at the beautiful people, I wrote postcards to send home.

I didn't do enough of that during my career.

* * *

Recently, I was having a cocktail on the back deck with my youngest son, Michael, who is appropriately using his psychology degree to work as a bartender at one of Toronto's most prestigious restaurants. Michael—I still call him "Little Mikey," even though he is twenty-six and stands six feet tall—came up with the moniker *Breakfast with Dave* more than twelve years ago. The two of us were sitting outside on a hot summer's day, and Mikey said, "Dad, have you ever been to Japan?"

"Many times."

"Did you like it?"

"Domo! Let's just say I loved it!"

"Can you tell me about your first trip there?"

My first trip to Japan was in 1996, while I was working for the economics department at BMO Nesbitt Burns. I was a young economist on his first major marketing trip. I was scheduled to meet with all the major banks, insurance companies, and mutual funds in Tokyo.

Before the trip, the heads of sales and trading in Toronto drilled me on Japanese culture and protocol.

My macro or market views seemed less important than conducting myself appropriately in meetings.

"Be sure to bow your head when you meet the executives."

"When they give you their business cards, stare at them for twenty seconds."

"When you give your talk, don't immediately discuss the markets;

instead, express your honor at being there and your appreciation for Japanese culture."

And for me, the most challenging, "Dave, speak slowly and in soft tones."

Countless other pieces of advice extended beyond the meetings:

"Don't count your change when making a transaction."

"Don't open taxi doors; the driver will do it for you."

I practiced *ohayo gozaimasu* and *sumimasen ga* in front of the mirror like a high school valedictorian (not that I would know). My superiors took me out for multiple sushi tutorials to teach me how to use chopsticks correctly. I love Japanese food and requested extra lessons.

My first day in Tokyo, I arrived at my hotel, the old Imperial, and quickly realized I could have used a few more cultural lessons. I was near the front of a packed elevator, filled with about ten men and one woman. We were going down. When the elevator door opened, I motioned for the woman to exit first. She just stood there. The men glared at me as they walked out. Then she practically pushed me out, and as she passed me in the lobby she gave me a glare. So much for my polite Canadian upbringing.

The real fireworks began at my first meeting with Japan's largest life insurance company. Beforehand, the BMO Nesbitt salesperson in Tokyo took me for a quick breakfast. He knew I was a rookie. He asked, "So the team in Toronto went through how to act in the Japanese culture?" I told him about my training. He seemed pleased and emphasized, "Stare at their cards, don't shake hands but bow your head, and when you start to talk, please don't launch into your pitch on bonds, stocks, the currency, and the economy. Spend the first ten minutes on how great your stay has been and what an honor it is to be in Japan." Yes, yes, I got it.

I did everything I was told: cards, bowing, niceties.

We were in a large, beautifully decorated room next to the CIO's office, about ten of us sitting on small chairs around a long rectangular table.

About ten minutes into my spiel, a woman walked in with a tray of ornate teacups, placed them in front of us, poured hot liquid into each, and left. I was in the zone, pontificating about the "house" view on everything macro and market.

At some point, maybe ten or fifteen minutes later, I noticed my sales guy staring at me with a scowl. Ten minutes after that, he was shooting daggers at me with his eyes. I had no clue what was happening, but I knew he was angry. I finished up, took questions, and honestly thought he was going to jump across the table and slap me.

With the meeting over, I said my goodbyes most respectfully. I had practiced my "*sayonara*" back home to a tee. And that turned out to be my major faux pas—tea.

In the elevator on the way down, the salesperson turned to me, rather furiously, and said, "What is wrong with you?"

"Why are you so angry with me? Do you disagree with my forecasts?"

"Didn't they teach you anything at headquarters?"

"To the point where I feel like a Samurai."

"Did you not notice that nobody at the table touched their green tea, not even a sip?"

"Come to think of it, you're right."

"Do you know why?"

I gulped, bracing myself. He yelled, and it was a good thing we were alone in the elevator. "Because the hosts can only have their sip of tea once the guest does! Because of you, they couldn't drink their tea!"

I shouldn't have responded with, "I don't even like green tea."

He didn't speak to me for the rest of the trip. Afterward, I kept asking myself, "Did I just blow the bank's century-long relationship with this life insurance company?"

When I arrived home, the only feedback I received from the senior brass at my firm was, "I heard about the tea incident." Good grief. I didn't have a chance to say *gomen nasai* to our hosts because I had no clue I was supposed to take the first sip of green tea. Why didn't anyone tell me that when they took me out for sushi? Maybe because we were all drinking Sapporo?

Lesson learned: always do your homework. Leave no stone unturned. And be sure to read the room. I found out later that everyone in the room was sending darts my way, not just the BMO salesperson.

One other thing I should mention about that first trip. When Rachael found out I was landing in Tokyo on a Saturday morning, with plenty of time to myself since my first meeting wasn't until Monday, she bought me a map, a book about Japanese culture and cuisine, and a Japanese-English translation dictionary (arigato!). I can still hear her saying, "There is no way you are going to spend your spare time holed up in your hotel room going over your slides. You are going to take this opportunity and explore a part of the world you never in your wildest dreams thought you would visit."

I took her sage advice. I walked for miles and also took the subway and made it to the Imperial Palace, Roppongi, and even the famous Tsukiji Fish Market, which housed the largest outside daily fresh tuna auction in the world. That was an over-the-top taste experience—fish and seafood that had just been caught at 5:30 that morning.

Those of us lucky enough to travel to exotic places as part of our job should take the time to take it all in. As Louis Armstrong put it, "What a wonderful world." Best not to miss out.

As for Little Mikey, I told him that Japan was a terrific choice, only keep it a personal trip and don't spend all your time in a boardroom.

CHAPTER 13

Get Everything in Writing

I beat out several candidates for the top economics and strategy job at Merrill Lynch Canada in early 2000. Among them was Jeff Rubin, who then held that dual role at CIBC in Toronto. He was the top-ranked economist in institutional client surveys, before being displaced by yours truly. Jeff's being passed over had nothing to do with his abilities: he was, and remains, an excellent economist and presenter. I was told the decision came down to his attitude. Jeff has a brashness, a bravado, and a sense of superiority that the senior leadership in New York detected. While regional senior leaders existed at Merrill, all decision-making occurred in New York. Every senior person at the various country levels had a dotted-line reporting relationship to someone at headquarters in the World Financial Center on Vesey Street.

Pleased to leave BMO Nesbitt Burns for Merrill, I was naive enough to think a verbal pledge and a handshake were enough. I'm not talking about my employment contract. It was about promises made but not kept by my manager in Toronto, who headed up the Canadian research team. Everyone in the regions, no matter the department, had a thick line of reporting locally and a thin one into somebody senior in New York City, the center of the universe.

The exceptional economist and strategist, Robert Spector, and a junior analyst, Scott Kinnear, who later climbed the senior ranks at the Bank of Canada, joined me from Nesbitt. My former boss and chief economist at the time, Sherry Cooper, was so furious with me that my office was quickly cleaned out and nobody at the bank was ever notified that I was gone, prompting the senior folks on the bond desk to openly complain. At one point, the CEO, Bill Downe, called me up to make a counter-offer: I would be chief economist of the institutional business while Sherry would have the same role for the wealth management department. I knew it would never work, and I was more than thrilled to join Merrill, which was the big leagues, so I politely turned down Bill's offer.

Robert Spector and I were given assurances by the head of research in Toronto that he would purchase Canadian databases for us to do our jobs. It didn't happen. We faced delays and obfuscation from the get-go. Weeks went by, with no Canadian data forthcoming. We were told to go to New York, spend time with the folks there who presided over international macro and market research, and see what Canadian data they had. After spending a few days in New York, groveling for data, we came back empty-handed.

I met with one of our bosses in Toronto, who told us he would begin the process of purchasing data for us. We knew who the vendors were, and they were more than willing to provide us with steep discounts. Still, it didn't happen. It reached a point where I was calling in favors from my Bay Street competitors, who were also friends, asking them to share their data with me on an ad hoc basis. They did, at their own peril. They saved me in those first few months, but it was difficult and embarrassing to have to beg for the data I needed to do my job. Another of my bosses thought it was great that I was getting data for free. The fact that I was relying on my rivals to bail me out was of little consequence.

Then came my savior. There was an evening when I was sitting at a desk on the trading floor, and I must have had a look of anguish on my face. Along came Doug Demartin, a Merrill veteran from New York who was parachuted in to run the entire Canadian fixed-income team after the legendary Paul Thomas had been promoted to co-run the global business out of Manhattan. Doug had a ton of pull in the building. He approached me and said, "Dave, why are you so downcast?" I told him exactly what had happened, and he was shocked. He patted me on the back and said, "Leave it with me. We have a senior management meeting tomorrow, and I'm putting this situation of yours in the agenda." For the first time in two months, I finally got a good night's sleep.

Two days later, contracts were signed with the external data vendors, and my troubles melted away. I asked Doug what happened at the meeting, and he told me all he had done was ask, "Why would we bother to hire a chief economist and strategist, and not give him the tools to succeed?"

From what I heard, one of my managers was excoriated. The very next day, he walked into my office, shut the door, and chewed me out for ten minutes. He told me I'd sold him out and accused me of going behind his back. He threatened me and left me with the strong impression that my days were numbered. I bit my tongue, knowing that, in the end, I'd got what I wanted.

It was another learning lesson. Two, actually. First, when you work at a big institution, be sure to find a sugar daddy who has influence. Second, forget handshakes—there is no replacement for getting what you need in writing.

CHAPTER 14
New York Calling

When I left BMO to join Merrill, it did not have a macro strategy team. That was part of the appeal: I had the opportunity to be a pioneer as the firm's first chief Canadian economist and strategist, not filling anyone's shoes. Robert Spector and I made our marks right away. We created a monthly actionable investment publication called Strategizer, which was a huge complement to my morning market memo. It was a huge home run with the firm's retail and institutional clients. In our first year, we were ranked third in the Brendan Wood annual survey of Canadian clients and never looked back. The following year, we ranked first. Things were going great.

Unbeknownst to me, our material was being read beyond Canada. A few years later, I was having lunch with Patrick Brady, head of Merrill's US institutional sales force, at our favorite Italian restaurant in Tribeca. He told me that one day in 2000 or 2001, Bob McCann, head of treasury operations at Merrill, was walking the trading floor and saw copies of *Canada: Morning Market Memo* scattered everywhere—on desks, chairs, the floor. According to Patrick, "Bob says, 'You guys are the US desk; why the hell are you reading this stuff from Canada?' Someone replied, 'Bob, everyone in the entire global system reads this guy. I'm surprised you don't." Few economists were then publishing daily reports that arrived before the start of the trading day. Apparently, Bob added himself to my distribution list shortly thereafter, and the senior leadership at Merrill had me on their radar.

In September 2002, I got a call from Bob McCann, who as one of the top three senior officials at Merrill oversaw research, sales, and trading. He asked if I would ever contemplate moving to New York. I was surprised at the question, but my adrenaline was running high. I said, "Sure, but why?" Bob didn't mince words: "You'll see. I just wanted to know if you'd ever be willing to make the move." And that was the conversation.

About two months later, the day before Thanksgiving, 2002, I heard my phone ring, saw the 212 area code flash, and my heart skipped a beat. Maybe thirty minutes earlier, senior management had announced a radical restructuring of the global research team. The US chief economist, Bruce Steinberg, was out. I picked up and it was Bob McCann again.

"Remember our conversation of two months ago?"

"I sure do."

"Did you see the announcement?"

"I sure did."

"In answer to your question as to why I wanted to know if you'd move to New York, it's because I want you to take on the role as the firm's new chief economist."

I can't remember if I fell off my chair, but I may well have.

"You interested?"

I think I responded with "yes!" before he'd even finished the question. I was told to clear out my calendar the following week to head to New York to be vetted by the head honchos. So it wasn't a gimme, but I was on top of the short list.

It was just past noontime that day and my heart was racing. Word got out that I was given an offer. Information spreads quickly in the financial markets. There was pandemonium on the trading floor. When I left my office, I was accosted. I literally ran out from the trading floor, yelling "Gotta run! Late for lunch with my folks." Which was the truth.

I arrived at least a half hour late to lunch. Mom and Dad were sitting there in the Old Spaghetti Factory on the outskirts of the Toronto financial district. My folks loved that spot—remember, they were Depression-era parents. They were sipping iced tea, not the least bit upset that I was tardy. Big smiles on their faces. They were just elated that I would take time out of my usual hectic day to eat with them. Now that they've both passed away, I wish I took them out for lunch way more often than I did. More on my struggles with work-life balance later. I still remember them beaming with pride when I told them the news. I mean a real beam. That look of immense pride sticks with me to this day.

* * *

I don't think I made it back to the office that day. On the way home, I bought a bottle of champagne. When I walked through the door, Rachael said, "What's the bubbly for?"

"Bruce Steinberg was fired and I basically got offered his job."

"In New York?"

To which I replied affirmatively.

"I feared this day would come." Rachael was wearing the exact opposite look that I'd seen on the faces of my parents.

Talk about a lead balloon. There were a range of health-related issues in the family, nothing serious but when it involves your kids, it's never unserious. That's why Rachael was despondent. We both knew she wasn't going to uproot the family, considering our personal circumstances, and move to New York.

I didn't uncork the champagne bottle that evening.

Instead, I poured myself a single malt (a few actually) and ruminated the entire night. I came to the conclusion that no way, no how was I going to leave my family. Not even for *that* job.

I called Bob McCann the following day and told him my situation. I wasn't going without my wife and boys. Meanwhile, the Canadian desk had already come up with a new nickname for me. I was no longer Rosie. I was 212.

The top guns in New York didn't take no for an answer. The next thing I knew, two senior Merrill officials who were responsible for the Americas were flying from New York to Toronto and set up a meeting with me. They were stunned that anyone would choose *not* to live in New York. I'm not entirely sure they were convinced that Rachael wouldn't make the trek to the center of the universe. They thought I was holding out for more money, so they came armed with a far more lucrative contract for me to sign. A lesson here for anyone in a job search: never accept the first offer; always remember that the first offer is rarely the final offer—everything is a negotiation.

That said, I wasn't looking for more pay. I was then told that Mother Merrill would pay for a one-bedroom apartment for me in Lower Manhattan and that I could fly back and forth between New York and Toronto at my discretion. On their dime.

I went back to Rachael with all this information. In her wisdom, she said, "Dave, they are sending you a very clear message that they want you for this job. So, if you don't accept the offer and decide to stay at Merrill, expect to be diminished and marginalized over time. They will also see you as a non-risk taker in an industry of risk, and that definitely will weigh against you. Then again, you can always quit and find something else in Toronto."

Rachael had done some nifty detective work and found that the typical chief economist at Merrill Lynch lasted a grand total of three years before being turfed. Even knowing that history, I wasn't dissuaded.

Rachael also offered me a middle ground. The decision, she said, was all mine, but that if I decided to accept the offer, I should consider it for two years and then come back home for good and monetize my Wall Street experience on Bay Street.

So, it was agreed. I would work in New York from Monday to Friday, put my family time in on the weekends, and engage in this new life for two years. I remember telling my three sons (aged three, six, and nine at the time) that I would be gone Monday to Friday going forward, but that on each trip back home I would bring them back lots of treats. They cheered and started to dance. Me? I was practically crying.

I never thought, at the outset, that I would be in New York for nearly seven years. I'm still surprised I survived as long as I did and wasn't fired for my cautious views as the market bubble formed and crested during my time there. The average lifespan of a chief economist was three years, as per Rachael's nifty detective work. And several senior people at the firm did take runs at me. I even faced a tribunal and an external consultant's 360-degree assessment. Somehow, I persevered.

But neither did I think my initial two-year timeline was realistic, because who deliberately wants to be an asterisk in history? And once I started getting ranked in the Institutional Investor annual rankings for Wall Street economists, and once I saw the massive bubble being built in the housing and credit market in the mid-2000s, the notion of leaving New York became increasingly unpalatable to me.

While I was back on the weekends, I was never really 100 percent present for my family. My head was in the clouds. I was always consumed with the coming Monday morning 7:30 a.m. macro/strategy call with the Merrill sales and trading team. This was the moment for everyone in my group to shine, the most important five minutes of the week. If my phone didn't start ringing by 8:00 a.m., I knew that I'd delivered a dud, or that what I had said had failed to resonate. But if a salesperson from the desk would call and say, "I have a PM [portfolio manager] from Citadel on the other line to talk about what you said this morning," I knew I'd hit a home run. I was fiercely competitive and was always trying to deliver something that nobody else was thinking about yet.

I readily admit that for seven years in the jungle, I neglected my family. It's not something I am proud of. It's one of my life's regrets. I still recall all too well putting Jacob, my middle son and today my COO, to bed on a Sunday evening, and him invariably asking me whether I was going to New York the next day. Every time I said yes, I would hear this guttural sigh. It pulls my heartstrings to this day.

If you asked me today if I would have done things differently, the answer is an unequivocal yes. My life in those years was far from normal, in so many respects. I remember how my dad once told me that the beauty of life and nature is that they constantly move into balance. I had no balance. Weekends at swimming lessons and Pizza Hut aside, I simply was not present for the kids. The number of soccer games and music recitals I missed is embarrassingly long. Guess how many parent-teacher interviews I've been to? The number is embarrassingly low. Zero.

At least the boys, now adults, forgive me for my prolonged absences. I always claimed that I was making all these sacrifices for them. That was an excuse for me not making a better attempt to have some balance in my life. I actually didn't sacrifice anything. I cheated them out of time with me in their youth as I outsourced parenthood to my wife. That's the harsh truth.

Those seven years in New York with me as an absentee father and husband were hard on Rachael. She, virtually on her own, was bringing up the boys in their formative years when nurturing, love, and attention are critical to a child's development. It is all because of Rachael that our three boys have become stellar people. I give her all the credit.

A few years ago, I recounted the whole story to a friend and former Merrill colleague over lunch (and wine) in Toronto. She, too, had climbed the ladder. She was on the derivatives team. She had a spouse who also was pursuing a successful business career of his own, while they were bringing up a young family. When I told her how Rachael responded to me breaking the news of the Merrill offer, saying, "I am happy for you, just not for me," my friend teared up and told me that was a plea not to accept the offer. She's right. But you can't turn back time.

The strains on my family life would reach a crescendo in the opening months of 2009. Rachael asked me bluntly: "What part of two and seven years do you not understand?" I remember answering, "I always told you I was bad at math." Despite being offered a promotion after Bank of America bought Merrill, with a ton more pay, staff, adding market strategy to my economics role, I resisted temptation and came home for good. I followed Bob Farrell's first rule on mean reversion and decided to mean-revert my life to balance out my career with my family responsibilities. And I must say it was a great decision.

Another lesson from all this: success in one's career requires sacrifice; just don't go to extremes like I did.

CHAPTER 15

Don't Get Stuck on the First Page

When I was promoted to chief economist at Merrill in New York, Candace Browning, who headed the firm's research effort—a position she still holds—gave me the option of discontinuing my daily report. She worried that the already-intense demands of my role would lead to burnout. And, truth be told, it was exhausting. But the daily had become such an integral part of my routine that I couldn't give it up. It kept me sharp and, importantly, benefited Merrill's trading and sales desks, the thundering herd of financial advisors, and our clients. While waking up at 4:00 a.m. was painful, I always enjoyed writing it (and still do, though I now sleep in until 4:30 a.m.!). When I arrived in New York, I simply renamed it Morning Market Memo. Not particularly snazzy, but I liked the alliteration.

Before I started in New York, the heads of equities and fixed income also asked if I would continue publishing the daily, as clients were requesting it. I replied, "Of course."

They followed with, "We understand you cover global topics, but remember, you represent Canada. We have economics teams in London, Tokyo, Paris, Frankfurt, and Mexico City, so please promise to keep your nose clean, stick to your knitting, and avoid stepping on their toes."

It was one of the few times I lied. I told them, "No problem." Sure thing.

That daily newsletter, which I started in 1998 at BMO Nesbitt under the title "Rosie's A.M. Tidbits" and which had garnered widespread attention in the Canadian investment industry, went viral at Merrill Lynch, with its huge global presence. There was no better feeling than getting a call from the equity and fixed income sales desk that went something like this: "Hey Rosie, I have the CIO from Fidelity on the line who wants more color on something you wrote in today's daily." Ironically, instead of creating animosity among my peers across the Merrill macro research platform, many of the regional analysts quoted my research in their publications.

I was relieved that when I arrived for my first day at Merrill Lynch on Wall Street in the autumn of 2002, the market didn't collapse 23 percent as it had on my first day on the job in Toronto. There was nevertheless plenty of turmoil and angst: we were in the wake of the tech bubble's bursting and the WorldCom and Enron accounting fiascos. But we were in the process of making an uneven transition from bear market to bull market, and better days were ahead.

What made my first day special was that I would, for the first time, be presenting to some of the world's most famous and venerable chief investment officers and portfolio managers. This was the big leagues. Merrill, at the time, was one of the largest and most influential investment banks and retail brokerage firms in the world. It sat alongside Goldman Sachs, Morgan Stanley, and Citigroup at the top of global finance, and was distinguished by its enormous network of financial advisors, known as "the thundering herd."

The first salesperson on the equity desk to take me on a marketing tour through Midtown Manhattan was Bob Cuillo, arguably the most seasoned and well-respected guy in the trading room. He had the best accounts, or at least a good chunk of them.

I was pumped. At the first meeting, it was me, Bob, the chief investment officer of one of the largest mutual funds in the United States, and about a dozen of his portfolio managers and research staff, all together in a stately boardroom. I handed out my chart package, and after a quick introduction about myself and my background, I launched in. I spent a minute or two on the first chart and was about to turn to the second when the CIO said, "Can you just go back to page one?" So, I did. I have to admit it was a bit of a convoluted graphic, a side-by-side with two or three lines on each attempting to drive home some causal relationship or another. I can't remember exactly what I was trying to demonstrate. And the CIO just kept asking more and more questions about the relationships. Why I chose this data for the charts, he wanted to know, and why didn't I use a log scale. Why had I used "real" instead of "nominal variables." He had issues with the legends. Every answer I gave was followed by another question to that answer, and on it went. Forty minutes on one innocuous graph. He seemed very confused, and I don't think my answers were making things any easier for him. I could feel my heart pounding through my chest and beads of sweat rolling from my temples. By the time the hour was up, I had made it to page three of a twenty-five-page slide show. It was over, and I had hardly begun.

As I rode the elevator down with Bob, the silence was deafening. We walked to Sixth Avenue for our second meeting, and just before we entered the building, Bob said, "Dave, I have some advice for you."

"What?"

"At this next meeting, just skip the first chart."

So I learned a valuable lesson that first day in Manhattan. Keep it simple! Forget about six lines on one page. As time went on, I decided to bring along a chart package for posterity's sake and just give a talk. If questions ever arose that a slide could speak to, I had what I needed. I am happy to report that after day one, I never again failed to get through my entire presentation. I'll forever be grateful to Bob for that advice.

It wasn't the last time the first page of a presentation got me in trouble. About five years later, I was asked by John Paulson, the famed hedge fund manager, to come to his office in midtown to observe one of his meetings with his advisory committee and stay for lunch after. I was marketing to institutional clients that day and had a free hour in between, so I accepted.

I had forty presentation packages with me for my afternoon meetings. What I didn't anticipate was John asking me to give a presentation to the group after lunch. I remember him saying, as clear as day, "and look, Dave even brought some presentation material for us." I didn't have the heart (or courage) to tell John that the presentations weren't for him.

Gary Shilling, one of John's external advisors, and a former Merrill Lynch chief economist, was at this committee meeting. We were (and are) good friends and share the same outlook on the economy and markets. Also sitting at this committee that day was the one and only Alan Greenspan, legendary chair of the Federal Reserve and arguably the most important voice in the world of economics at the time.

Why this matters is because my very first slide was a cheeky picture of Alan Greenspan blowing bubbles. The title was "Serial Bubble Blower." In my life, I've never spent so much time talking before flipping through my presentation. I could see others around the table who'd flipped to that first slide begin to chuckle and snicker as they glanced over at the maestro. I was freaking out inside.

The thing is, Greenspan's eyes were closed. At first, I thought it was just temporary, but his eyes stayed shut the entire time. I don't know if he was asleep or meditating, but he didn't open his eyes until the end of my presentation. He never saw the unflattering caricature, or any other slide, for that matter, and I made sure to take his copy of the chart package away from him, saying I needed it for my next meeting.

I dodged a bullet with Greenspan. The lesson is to skip the first slide altogether.

CHAPTER 16

New York State of Mind

Working as chief economist at Merrill Lynch in New York put me in the ranks of its several illustrious economists, including Gary Shilling, Jack Lavery, and Donald Straszheim. It was an honor to be there, but I later found out I was not the top choice for the job, after all. Despite how much the leadership in New York had wanted me for the job, I was actually a placeholder. All eyes were on the number two of my recently dismissed predecessor, the former chief economist Bruce Steinberg. Frankly, everyone across the organization thought the number two was the heir apparent, but the research leadership thought he needed seasoning, especially with regard to marketing and penetrating the client base. They saw how my research resonated with the Canadian client base—my feedback into New York in just two years was stellar.

I was never told that I was only hired to blaze the trail for my successor and groom this person for the firm's top macro job. When I departed for New York in late 2002, my second-in-command, the consistently reliable Robert Spector, assumed my former role as head of economics and strategy for Merrill Canada. While he still reported to me, this was a significant advancement for him. He later informed me that during his interviews in New York, which I had believed were solely for his vetting, the inquiries focused more on David Rosenberg and whether I could effectively collaborate with Steinberg's number two in the US economics department. This revelation reminded me of Rachael's research indicating that Merrill

Lynch had a three-year clock on its chief. My dear friend Gary Shilling recounts his experience of being fired twice in a single decade.

I was not told what brought about Bruce Steinberg's demise. Rumor had it that he orchestrated a coup, undermining his boss from behind the scenes. Despite Merrill's reputation as a close-knit work environment, such behavior was not uncommon. Before the dismissal of another of our predecessors, Donald Straszheim, there were press leaks suggesting that the heads of research at Merrill were considering hiring Ed Yardeni in his stead. Ed, a well-known name, reportedly demanded too much creative freedom, leading to Bruce Steinberg's appointment.

While I liked Bruce, I never found his team's research particularly innovative; it generally mirrored the consensus view and offered little beyond what was already available in the *Wall Street Journal.* Don's work, by contrast, was excellent. However, there was a lot of talk in the corridors about his frequent absences due to golfing with financial advisors. He struggled to fully support the institutional sales force, a crucial factor that can significantly impact an analyst's, strategist's, or economist's success.

My time on the trading floor in my younger years at the Bank of Nova Scotia and BMO Nesbitt Burns proved invaluable at Merrill. Moreover, Robert Spector and I had been situated right on the cavernous sales and fixed-income trading floor at Merrill Canada, ensuring constant contact with market makers. Many economists fear traders, and often wind up the target of their jokes and ridicule. The key to confronting that fear is engagement: answer their questions, provide valuable information for their clients, and show them genuine interest. Ultimately, the academic credentials required to become a street economist can be intimidating to those on the sales and trading desk, which may explain their condescending behavior toward the resident economist. Besides, in forecasting, you're bound to be wrong more often than right, much like even the best home run hitter in baseball. Economists make so many predictions that everyone accumulates a long list of inaccurate forecasts, making us easy targets.

If you want to survive in this jungle, the trick is to be indispensable to those who generate revenue. So brush off the ridicule and abuse, and invite the trader for coffee or a beer. Building friendships is a worthwhile investment of your time. Salespeople are on the front lines and are the best source of information regarding client concerns. Ultimately, we are all responsible to the client base, regardless of our role. Many economists, isolated in ivory towers, seem unaware of who they ultimately serve.

In the end, this is what led to my predecessor Bruce Steinberg's demise. I was told by people on the Merrill sales and trading desk that success had gone to his head and that he had become inaccessible. He even spent summers working from his home in the Hamptons, which is ill-advised in a role that demands constant client attention, especially considering that, back then, virtual meetings with clients via Teams or Zoom were not an option. You were either in their office, or you were somewhere else.

Bruce also overstayed his bullish call on the late 1990s tech bubble, but that wasn't really why he lost his job. It didn't help, but people close to him told me that his lack of a relationship with the sales force was the real problem, because when things got tough, nobody was around to advocate for him to Bob McCann. I know firsthand, having faced the firing squad myself several times, how critical it is to have the support of the people who actually bring in the money. I called them the silent majority because there was always a vocal minority ready to criticize me for not being bullish enough.

* * *

When I arrived in New York, one of the first things I did was call a lunch meeting with staff. It's important to note that there were two US economics departments in New York when I arrived, not one. One was dedicated to the equity desk, formerly led by Bruce Steinberg, and the other catered to the fixed-income business, led by the excellent economist Marty Mauro. The setup was excessive. These two teams not only produced research with divergent views, but also had completely divergent sets of economic forecasts. To make matters worse, the members of each team detested each other.

I already knew all of this before I moved to Manhattan. The economists and strategists across the global Merrill system were well known to one another. We had frequent conference calls and offsites. I knew everyone on Bruce's team and Marty's team intimately. I always thought Marty's team did better work, but to be honest, neither team ever gave me a spark of inspiration, nothing I could market back to clients on Bay Street. I just marketed my own view on the US economy and markets and hoped my superiors wouldn't find out that I was going rogue. I had no qualms about being a contrarian, when the times were right, and publishing differentiated research. That was not how things were being done in New York, although it changed when I got there.

Immediately on arriving in New York, I called a lunch meeting with staff. Pizza and beer. It's important to note the major reorganization of the research department that included Bruce Steinberg's departure and involved a merger of the two separate economic units. Several other employees had been let go to save costs and reduce redundancy. However, Merrill left me with a department that was still too large, and some of those who survived the cuts were not people I would have retained. I'd had no say in the matter. I was instructed to give the newly merged department a chance. After a year, I was advised, I would have the latitude to start making personnel changes if I felt any were necessary.

Ultimately, nobody who started with me at Merrill in New York in 2002 was still there when I left in 2009. Along the way, we went from a sixth-place ranking in the II survey at the outset to second place by 2008, second only to Ed Hyman at International Strategy and Investment Group. That suggests that I made the right personnel changes. Some people quit because they didn't appreciate my work ethic or competitive drive, while others were simply let go because they didn't understand the vision.

I don't mean to sound harsh, but what I realized at that first lunch was that the economics department had been run like a *de facto* country club. There was no sense of urgency within the group. I wouldn't necessarily call them lazy, but most weren't hard-working, and to a large extent, everybody took their jobs and Merrill's status for granted. When I found out that nobody at the equity economics department ever stepped onto the trading floor—not Bruce, and not his number two (or his number three, four, or five)—I was nearly apoplectic. This was the dominant economics department, the one dedicated to the equity sales and trading force, and no one ever visited the trading floor. At least Marty Mauro's team had a desk economist, Mary Dennis, who was excellent and revered on the sales and trading desk. But on Bruce's team, no one even knew the name of a single senior trader or salesperson. I was astonished.

At that lunch, I pulled a General Patton and read out the new rules for success. First and foremost, someone, including me, had to be on the desk for at least an hour a day—over and above the desk economist role. We needed to walk around the floor, talk to the traders and sales force, answer their questions, and show them attention, just as I'd done in Toronto for many years. I was never any smarter than any other economist in terms of analysis, but I was effective in efficiently communicating our information, which meant face-to-face contact as opposed to relying on people to actually read our output. Like Woody Allen said, 80 percent of success is showing up. I couldn't believe that for so many years, nobody from the economics team had been showing up on the trading floor.

The other change involved the actual research. I told the disgruntled team—remember, it wasn't just the shock of having a new boss, but the fact that these two merged teams couldn't stand each other—that the days of hugging the consensus, producing research that was accessible elsewhere, and feeding clients pablum were gone. I pledged to lead by example. I totally revamped the suite of products and ensured that all our economic calls had a market call attached to them. For instance, it wasn't enough to say the economy was heading into recession; the next step was to buy treasuries and reduce equity exposure. Be relevant and understand who our clients are! I told them our goal needed to be that portfolio managers and investors would yearn for our material to such an extent that they wouldn't go home on a Friday afternoon until they printed our research.

I emphasized that while we needed to have point forecasts, with specific numbers for GDP or CPI forecasts, much of that was just maintenance. It might be necessary, but it would not improve our ranking. Producing innovative and unique research was far more important. We couldn't afford to be a commodity—I repeated that often. If we published excellent, pertinent, but also unconventional research, clients would forgive us when our calls went awry, or at least give us time. From my vantage point in Toronto, as a consumer of US macro research, I never found that the Merrill team in New York was producing innovative research or making itself accessible. Robert Spector and I had consistently published hard-hitting research that couldn't be replicated elsewhere—it's an ethos I live by to this day.

I was consumed by the idea of creating an economics department constantly focused on what lies ahead, confident that we would be rewarded for it. We would know we were on the right track when, despite a losing streak on our calls, I was still filling the room at client lunch and dinner events because they felt compelled to hear what I had to say. If you can fill a room even when your call is not working out, that's when you have become a marquee player in this business. The worst thing is to be ignored, and I had a plan to ensure that would never happen to me or my team. It simply required the courage to be thought-provoking and a refusal to let the consensus shape our views and convictions.

Managing the merged department was tricky in those early days. Sadly, Mary Dennis stepped down from her role during my second year in New York. Her constant battles with the senior members of Bruce's macro team, as I was told in her exit interview, had worn her down. I was compelled to support the number two I had inherited from Bruce while simultaneously placating Mary because, frankly, she was more vital to my business than he was. She got fed up anyway and left to become a real estate agent. While I have not seen her since, I strongly believe she could have been the only one from the beginning to have stayed with me to the end if she had chosen to.

CHAPTER 17

Sew What?

I've struggled with my weight for the better part of the last thirty years. Second and even third helpings at a buffet were natural for me over the decades. And that doesn't even begin to cover my love for cherry cheesecake, fudge brownies, pecan pie, and tiramisu.

During my years at Merrill Lynch, from 2002 to 2009, I wined and dined clients practically every night. The wine alone likely exceeded my daily calorie allowance. I ballooned to well over 250 pounds, making sure I was both seen and heard. A trip to Boston during my later years at the bank proved to be an inflection point, setting me on the path to a vigorous weight-loss program. But it took a truly embarrassing episode to get me there.

After a busy day of marketing, I had an hour to relax in my hotel room before a keynote dinner address. As I reached for the door, I dropped some papers from my file folder. Bending over to pick them up, I heard a very loud rip. It was one of those Wile E. Coyote moments, just before he looks down. As I stood up, a sense of "uh oh" washed over me. I checked what happened, and my pants had split.

This wasn't some little tear. The fabric had ripped from my derrière to my crotch, at least twelve inches. Of course, I had only brought one suit to Boston.

The rip was impossible to disguise. And I had barely an hour before I needed to deliver my dinner speech in the hotel ballroom. Frantic doesn't even begin to describe my state. So, I ran downstairs, grabbed a cab, and quickly got my executive assistant, Francine, on the phone. I explained what happened. She conferenced in Andy Winton, a Merrill salesperson and good friend, to help us out. Andy started suggesting nearby tailor shops, but since it was well after 5:00 p.m., each was closed. It was hard to hear him, as I recall, because he kept erupting in gales of laughter between suggestions. Thanks, Andy! With no way to hide the tear in my trousers, I began to think I might have to deliver the speech in my hotel bathrobe.

Andy located a clothing repair shop, open for another half hour, not far from the hotel. The cab driver, amused by the situation, sped there. We arrived at a mom-and-pop shop, run by an elderly Chinese couple in an unglamorous part of downtown. They helped me immediately. There was no changing room, so I stood in the shop in my shoes, shirt, and jacket—but no pants.

As I stood there in my underwear, thinking, "Thank God it's late and this shop is about to close," three women walked in. I turned beet red, but my embarrassment was overshadowed by concern that I wouldn't make it to my speech—at least, not with my slacks on.

The husband did yeoman's work, stitching the pants within thirty minutes. Because he spoke little English, he had his daughter interpret, telling me under no circumstances to sit. Sitting, she said, would tear the stitches. She added that the suit was essentially ruined, with a shelf life of that evening only—and only if I remained standing. I wondered, "If I can't sit in the cab on the way back to the hotel, how will I get back?"

I got into a taxi and, as I slid into the back seat, pulled my pants down to my ankles. I kid you not.

Back at the hotel, I hurried to the ballroom, relieved I wasn't late. Unbeknownst to me, I was seated at the head table before my speech. I went on stage but ate my meal standing. The senior Merrill banker introducing me asked me to sit and eat. I said, "I pulled a muscle in my back, so I can't sit." Good thinking.

So there I was, before about 500 people, on stage, eating while standing. Slightly less embarrassing than being semi-clothed in the tailor shop, but still a very weird look. At least I didn't drop any food on my shirt.

I gave the speech, fielded questions at the bar afterward, and then headed back to my hotel room. My flight back to New York was the next morning, and I knew I'd have no choice but to sit on the airplane. Of course, as soon as I did, the stitches burst and the gaping rip in my trousers re-emerged. All I could do was pray I wouldn't see anyone I knew at the airport when I landed, especially nobody from the media.

I went straight to my apartment, changed suits, and headed to the office. By that point, the story had gone viral across the Merrill system, and everyone had a good laugh at my expense. Those Boston sales folks—such good friends, right?

Nobody laughed harder than Francine, who, at my goodbye party when I left Merrill in the spring of 2009, got up to speak and recounted that evening in Boston. She brought the house down, I have to admit. Even I found myself in tears.

Always travel with more than one suit when on business. Second, diet! Which I did. Trouser splits meant no more banana splits for yours truly. I ended up dropping thirty pounds in the next six months, so something good came out of that bizarre episode.

The final lesson is laugh at yourself. And while you do, try to find the silver lining, and make sure the lining in your pants is made of wool, not cotton.

CHAPTER 18

Strangers Bearing Gifts

Challenging bosses are a fact of life in any line of work, and I use the word "challenging" politely. I was fortunate to have had no problems with Warren Jestin and Aron Gampel in my early years at the Bank of Nova Scotia. They were elite and dedicated to their craft. They could be difficult to please, at times, but what boss isn't? The difference was that it was all about the work, not their egos, or other agendas.

When I left Merrill Canada in Toronto for Merrill in New York in late 2002, I had to say goodbye to one of the best bosses I had in my forty-year career, Ihor Danyliuk. Initially an analyst on the equity research team, Ihor moved into management and, in my final year in Toronto, headed the entire department. He understood that each research analyst was essentially running their own business and avoided micromanaging. He offered guidance and advice, not direction. Even when you were wrong on a call, he never breathed down your neck, but encouraged you to challenge yourself in a supportive way. After the Canadian research division was eliminated, he left Merrill and continued his senior research role at the National Bank of Canada. I learned a great deal from Ihor about effective people management and how to get the most out of a team. I'm not sure how effective I was at implementing those learnings—that's best left for those who worked for me to say. I am definitely not everyone's cup of tea.

I didn't realize how much I missed Ihor until my first few months in New York in 2003. As I was finding my footing, I was dealing with a disgruntled, merged team of economists who were stunned that this outsider was their new leader. I was also getting to know the vast network of sales and trading staff on the institutional desk across the United States, as well as the top financial advisors on the wealth management team—the thundering herd. There were hundreds of names and faces to remember, and that was before we got to the client base. Everything in the United States is Canada times ten, so the law of large numbers was truly in play. I was in equal parts excited and overwhelmed.

I was less enthused about my new reporting line. I won't name names—let's use My Boss—but this individual rose from relative obscurity within Merrill to head the entire global macro team. I knew this person, though not well. On visits to Toronto once or twice a year to see clients, this person would give a lunch presentation. I, as chief Canadian economist and strategist, barely registered. I don't even think this newly appointed head of Merrill research remembered having met me before I moved to New York. As a regional specialist in the Merrill system, you were basically a peon, even compared to the junior staff in New York, the center of the universe.

My Boss had a well-deserved reputation as a fine senior research strategist, but I knew that many of the people who reported to them were less than enamored with their management skills. We're talking the antithesis of Ihor. That quickly became obvious when I was openly disparaged because of intense disagreement with my initial forecasts in early 2003. I was just getting my feet wet, but it felt like cement was being poured on them. My Boss was always a major cheerleader for the US economy and enamored with the S&P 500. For as long as I can recall, My Boss was a bond bear and interest rate hawk, while I, from the Lacy Hunt and Gary Shilling school, had a bond-bullish bias. Instead of just allowing me to hang myself with my own rope, I was badgered constantly and pressured, right out of the gates, to change my interest rate and GDP forecast. The constant attempts to embarrass and shame me into changing my call didn't sway me one bit, although I knew I was paying a price. There was chatter, in those first six months, that I was going to be replaced.

I was never sure how My Boss catapulted into the enormous managerial responsibility of heading up all of global research at Merrill Lynch. That was an even bigger move up the ladder than mine. But as time went on, I noticed My Boss's superior, Bob McCann, spent more and more time in My Boss's office, and I observed how they interacted with each other. They had developed a close and cozy relationship. Bob was loved by some and feared by all. He was one of the top three most important figures at Merrill. My Boss's ability to hold Bob's ear made me question my longevity (even though it was Bob who blazed the trail for my promotion to New York). I kept thinking of what Rachael had said before I left. I worried that I would be the one to pull the median lifespan of a Merrill Lynch economist down to two years from three. Fortunately, Bob was receiving positive early feedback from the sales and trading desk about how refreshing it was to have a chief economist work the floor, which we were doing daily after years of neglect. It helps to be present.

Still, I wasn't untouchable. Nobody is. My Boss clearly wanted to get rid of me. There was no backing from on high, so the badgering continued. I was once taken out for dinner by My Boss. It was surprisingly pleasant until we were halfway through the main course. Then, My Boss relentlessly urged me to change my call on the Fed. I should have known that dinner was less about getting to know me and more about pressuring me to alter my view, despite the disclaimer on every report I published stating that I firmly believed in what I was sending out to clients. Every analyst needed this disclaimer after all the shenanigans that came to light in the recent tech bubble, when some analysts said one thing in private and another in public. I didn't bend. My Boss got so upset with me that the waiter was called and the bill was paid. I was abandoned at the table halfway through dinner. There was still a half bottle of Cabernet left, which I happily consumed.

As for my number two on the macro team, I couldn't help but notice that this person and My Boss had also become very close. I also knew that they were aligned in their market and macro views, which significantly differed from mine. By this time, I'd heard from Robert Spector about how senior management was concerned how I'd get along with my number two and if we could work together. I put the pieces together and realized that I was indeed a placeholder. This person would take over the economics department after benefiting from my tutelage on connecting with the client base, both internally and externally. Apparently, the only obstacle preventing this person from having my job was a lack of communication and marketing skills. He was the heir apparent, and it was increasingly clear that both my number two and the higher-ups were in a hurry for him to take his rightful place leading the economics function.

It took me a while to piece all this together, but I'd had an inkling at the start. During my first week on the job in New York, my number two walked into my office, signed an econometrics textbook that he'd published years earlier when he was pursuing his PhD at an Ivy League school, and handed it to me. "Dave," he said, "this is a gift from me to you." The phrase "beware of strangers bearing gifts" seemed particularly apt at that moment. When I recounted the story to Rachael back in Toronto the following weekend, she immediately said, "Dave, keep your eye on that guy."

As mentioned, I noticed that My Boss and my second-in-command were spending increasing amounts of time together. I didn't appreciate what that meant for me until I returned from my first marketing trip to the Southeast with the equity and fixed-income sales team. I was heavily focused on marketing at the time, aiming to raise my profile, promote my department, and share our newly developed views on the economy and markets. Consequently, I spent far more time with the sales force than with my own team during that first month. I reasoned that with several senior economists, long-time Merrill employees, and a reliable second-in-command, I could trust them to manage the department while I was away in the trenches.

I was gone for most of the week. Upon returning to Toronto to resume my role as part-time family man, I received a call from one of my junior economists—one of the few stellar performers on the team.

"Dave," he asked, "are you aware of what happened last week while you were traveling?"

"No."

"Your number-two was going around to everyone on the team to sign a petition to throw you out and have you replaced with him."

He added, "I didn't sign and there is nobody I know who did, but I'm surprised I'm the first to tell you this. You, we, have a problem on our hands. And you are simply away far too much, as an aside."

This junior economist was always direct, and I appreciated his honesty, his willingness to share his opinions, and his exceptional work ethic.

That weekend, I called a few other team members who verified the incident. Nobody had signed the petition. Although I was not even a year into the job, I had to deal with my first management crisis. What bothered me most was that it took time away from what I loved to do, and still love to do: read, analyze data, write reports, and communicate my findings to the client base.

When I flew into New York City the following Monday morning, I confronted my heir apparent in my office. This person admitted to what had transpired, and was more upset that nobody signed the petition than feeling guilt about it. To reiterate, I had been a little wary, especially since this second-in-command was so chummy with My Boss, who despised me. When I discussed the situation with My Boss, this person seemed depressed. Again, more sad that nobody had signed the petition than about me finding out.

My Boss asked, "What do you intend to do about it?"

"I think we, as in me and you, need to do respond forcefully because this was an insurrection while I was away busting my butt for the firm and if it goes unpunished, it will set a very bad precedent."

"Okay, then, what should we do?"

I said that I was going to sit down with HR and recommend that my second-in-command be put on probation, and that is exactly what happened.

However, this person didn't get fired. When it came time for bonuses, at my meeting with my direct report, after going through everyone in my department, this individual asked, "So what do we do with your number two?"

Like Al Pacino in *Godfather II*, I said, "Nothing," omitting the "senator" part. As in, this person would get nothing. My Boss unleashed some expletives at me but knew that if they overruled me, I would take it up with Bob McCann and see where the cards would fall. Next, my boss asked a setup question regarding the amount in the bonus pool I had originally planned for my so-called right-hand person: "What would you like to do with that excess in the bonus pool?"

I had always thought that my real second-in-command, Robert Spector in Toronto, was underpaid, so I recommended that the money that would have gone to my New York counterpart be diverted to Robert. My manager nixed that idea, decided to give the money to a team member that this person used to manage, and a few months later, Robert resigned and went to McLean Budden (a buy-side firm that has since been acquired by MFS Investment Management).

Two key lessons from this experience. First, always stay true to your word and never sell out. Second, if you ever find yourself in a position where you are given a number two or right-hand person, speak out and suggest that you either want to bring in your own person or at least set up interviews for the role to give yourself options.

Weeks before leaving for New York, I'd sought advice from Warren Jestin, the chief economist at the Bank of Nova Scotia. I had worked for him for seven years in the late 1980s and early 1990s. He had decades of successful team management under his belt and he is one of the most respected economists I have ever met. I needed to tap into that wisdom, so I asked him, "What is the most important thing I should be aware of as I embark on this new role in New York?" He immediately responded, "Make sure you find a strong number two, someone you can trust." Wise words. As a side note, Aron Gampel had been Warren's strong number two for many years and was incredibly loyal to him.

I'm happy to report that for the past six years, I have had the best right-hand man anyone could ask for. His name is Jacob Rosenberg.

CHAPTER 19

There Will Be Blood

In my entire ten-year tenure at Merrill Lynch, no other institutional client captured my heart—and tested my theses—more than the brilliant markets team at the Kuwait Investment Authority (KIA), the world's oldest sovereign wealth fund. Established in 1953, it oversees over $1 trillion in global assets. I don't think there was a trip to London when I didn't find myself in their offices, providing them with my often-provocative views. Let me say that not only was the investment team among the sharpest I have ever had the pleasure of meeting, but they were always the most hospitable. Very courteous people, always respectful without demurring, and I typically left the meetings a lot more knowledgeable than when I entered the room.

I started a great relationship with them early in my time at Merrill Canada, and I recall one meeting all too well when we debated the direction of the oil price. They were bullish. I was bearish (surprise, surprise). We each laid out our case, and neither side backed down. I was there with Derek Reisky, a Merrill sales guy, and Vikram Rao, the head of fixed-income trading out of Toronto. By that point, I had met with the KIA several times, and Derek, who always attended these gatherings, knew how comfortable I was with the KIA chief investment officer and his entire team. This was Vik's first meeting and as the disagreement over the oil price intensified, I could see him turning red and shooting daggers at me.

After the meeting, we headed down the elevator and Vik ripped into me. He really let off steam during that forty-floor descent. "You're telling the Kuwaitis where the oil price is going? That is their primary business. How can you possibly challenge them on something like this?" I've left out the expletives. I simply said, "Well, they asked, and I answered." I left it at that because Vik was not someone you wanted to anger. Plus, he was bigger than me.

As it turned out, KIA was correct, and I was wrong. Vik had a point: it's important to stick to your knitting in the forecasting business and don't pretend to know more about a subject than someone whose primary business is that exact topic.

But the story doesn't end there. As I said, I saw the KIA regularly. A few years later, sometime in the winter or spring of 2002, I made another trip with Derek to London. I never needed an excuse to fly to London, and at one point in the late 1990s, while at BMO Nesbitt Burns, I was offered a senior economics posting there.

I arrived early for the meeting and found Derek waiting alone in the lobby. The view of the city was spectacular. I was juggling twelve presentation packages in one hand and my BlackBerry in the other—it's amazing how ubiquitous those devices once were. The administrative assistant appeared and announced, "The team will see you now in the main boardroom." As I turned from the window and headed toward the boardroom, I failed to see a hard glass coffee table that was low to the floor. I walked right into it. I fell forward; my presentations and Blackberry went flying as I crashed headfirst into the table. It's a miracle the glass didn't shatter—but I certainly did. My head was bleeding. I stood up to find Derek looking utterly shocked. The assistant fetched the chief investment officer, who escorted me to the washroom and helped me clean up. I was still bleeding, so I asked for a towel, which he quickly provided.

Emerging from the men's room with my presentations in one hand and the towel pressed against my forehead—I'd given my phone to Derek—the CIO asked, "What are you doing?"

"I'm going to get this presentation started," I replied.

He looked as shocked as Derek had earlier. "Oh, no," the CIO said, "we'll postpone this until your next trip. Look at you, you're bleeding!"

"I've come too far and have too much to say to pass up this opportunity," I insisted. "A little blood isn't going to stop me."

So, I delivered the slide show, clicker in one hand, bloodied towel in the other, as if nothing had happened. I have never seen so many people look so aghast, not even in all the presentations I gave five years later about the bursting housing bubble's impact on the markets.

When we finished out, Derek and I headed from the KIA office to Heathrow. We were on a weeklong marketing trip through Europe, the usual one-city-per-day tour. Our next stop was Milan. It was mid-afternoon and we were scheduled to land in Italy in the early evening. In the black car—the good old days of the black cars!—Derek looked at the gash on my forehead and said, "We have time. We should stop by the Merrill office before heading to the airport to have that looked at." I didn't argue. The cut was pretty bad. The bleeding had stopped but my shirt and tie were a mess. Fortunately, the Merrill offices in London, like the tower on Vesey Street in New York, had a doctor's office. We arrived just after 4:00 p.m., after the doctor had already left, but the nurse saw me, put a stent in above my eyebrow, and said, "You're going to need stitches, so go straight to the closest hospital to your hotel when you land in Milan."

I thanked her, and we headed for Heathrow once again. I have to hand it to Derek. On the drive, he was on the phone trying to find a doctor at the hotel (there wasn't one) and then searched for hospitals near the hotel (there weren't any). After we landed in Milan, Derek took my bags to the hotel, and I went straight to a hospital about five miles away. The stent wasn't built to last and I started to bleed again. Even so, after arriving at the emergency room, I sat in the waiting room for three or four hours before anyone saw me. I must have used six boxes of Kleenex. Sitting in the

ER late into the night, watching patient after patient being wheeled in on gurneys, covered in blood, I stopped feeling sorry for myself—were these people all shot?

I finally saw the medical staff. Despite the fact that they didn't speak English, they knew exactly what to do. They put in six dissolvable stitches, and I was back in my hotel by 3:00 a.m.

When I finally got to my room and undressed, I looked at my body and saw bruises everywhere. The adrenaline had been running so high, and my forehead had such a gash, that I only then realized how much I ached. I was a ghastly sight. The stitches over my left eye made me look like a shorter version of Frankenstein.

My first meeting was a breakfast in the conference room at 9:00 a.m. Again, the Europeans do these things right; back home, they'd start closer to 7:00 a.m. Still, I only got four hours of sleep. People at the meeting looked astonished when they saw me. I told them "the last client didn't like my forecast."

The healing process took a long time. Throughout the week, my face looked worse, and my entire body hurt. My bruises turned from blue to purple. I wish the story ended there, but it doesn't.

* * *

A few months later, I noticed a lump on the right side of my neck. It grew bigger and bigger. I hoped it was nothing and would simply disappear. At the gym, on the treadmill, I'd gaze at this ever-larger lump in the big mirror in front of me. Shaving in the morning, it started to look like a golf ball. I'd take my shirt off at home to gauge Rachael's reaction, but she didn't seem concerned, so I figured maybe I shouldn't be so worried about this twin growing on my neck. Had to be nothing. But the lump kept growing, and I wondered when it would morph from a golf ball into a baseball. I considered giving it a name.

I finally realized I couldn't ignore it any longer. At work, I asked my senior lieutenant, Robert Spector, to step into a vacant office. "Don't worry," I said. "I'm not making a pass at you, but I need to take my shirt off and show you something." I'll never forget his face: pure shock.

"How long have you had this?"

"I don't know, two months maybe."

"You have to get this looked at right now!"

I called my regular physician, but he couldn't see me and recommended I go straight to the local clinic downtown near my office.

So I went. The doctor at the clinic, fresh out of school, barely in his twenties, ran some tests and scheduled a follow-up visit. Over the next week, I saw him three more times. During the last session, he asked, "Have you been seriously ill recently?" I said no. In fact, beyond the occasional sniffle, I rarely get sick. (Even when I had COVID-19 back in 2021, it was a one-day event. I still managed to do two client conference calls and my usual webcast.) The young doctor then sat me down and explained that he had run all sorts of tests and ultrasounds to rule things out. "After eliminating every other possible cause for this lump," he said bluntly, "I'm left with one conclusion: you have lymphoma, though I can't yet determine which type."

Well, that was unexpected. A few days later, I was scheduled for a biopsy at the oncology ward of Toronto General Hospital. As it happened, Rachael found the ultrasound receipt in my suit pocket while doing laundry that week. "What's this for?" she asked. I hadn't wanted to worry her, so she was completely unaware of what was happening until that moment. I told her everything, and as I did, I pulled up my shirt and showed her the golf ball-sized lump. "You never noticed this alien growing out of my neck for months?" I asked. I've never seen such astonishment on her face. But in the days that followed, she was her usual brave self, constantly trying to soothe my concerns, although I later discovered she was freaking out inside.

As for me, I just tried to block it all out and focus on my job. At least that would keep my mind off things. It was a useful strategy, similar to how I coped during the peak of the 2008–09 financial crisis, when nobody knew if they would have a job the next day. I've always been adept at compartmentalizing my thoughts, blocking things out, and not feeling sorry for myself.

I went for the biopsy expecting another young doctor. Instead, I had one who must have been well into his seventies. As I sat shirtless on the gurney, he inserted the needle into my lump, which now resembled a basketball. I thought, surely even this old guy couldn't miss such a large target. But as he stuck the needle in to retrieve the sample, he yelled, "Holy shit! Holy shit!" He ran to the counter, grabbed a box of Kleenex, and began wiping my neck.

"Holy shit good, or holy shit bad?" I asked.

"Your lump is collapsing!" he said.

"What?"

He said that he still needed to send the sample to the lab, but if it were cancerous, it wouldn't have collapsed as completely as it did. "Have you been seriously ill these past few months?" he asked. I said that the doctor at the clinic had asked the same thing weeks ago, and the answer was still no. Displaying his experience and wisdom, this doctor said, "Okay, let me rephrase that: have you had a bad accident or injury at any time these past few months?"

I told him about the KIA spill in London.

"What probably happened is that you ended up developing a blood clot," he said. This was confirmed the week after the biopsy.

"You travel a lot for work, right?" the doctor asked.

I confirmed that I did, and that I had just returned from Seattle two weeks prior.

"You don't have cancer, but let me tell you, that blood clot could have caused an aneurysm at any time, especially while you were in flight. Are you aware of the danger you put yourself in, even with this thing being benign?"

That hit me like a ton of bricks.

It's a bit of a gruesome tale, but it adds to the path of learning. The lessons are obvious: don't delay seeking medical help at the first sign of trouble, and don't board an airplane with a growth on your neck.

Apart from heeding this advice, I wouldn't change a thing. I think it's important to stay focused and avoid distractions. This is true in almost any profession. Despite the pain and bleeding, I completed my obligations, finished the London presentation to KIA, and the rest of my trip. I believe a chief economist on Wall Street should emulate an NFL quarterback—leave it all on the field. Take the hits, figuratively and literally, and understand that nothing matters more than the client.

CHAPTER 20

Missing Clues in Atlanta

During my first year as Merrill Lynch's chief economist, in early 2003, I was marketing in the US Southeast for both the fixed-income and equity teams. This was the same trip during which my right-hand person was busy back in New York trying to get me ousted. I was in Atlanta for one jam-packed day with eight meetings from dawn to late afternoon. In the early evening, a black car drove me to an incredibly well-groomed luxury private golf course just outside Atlanta. The fixed-income team was hosting a golf day for its top twenty clients. I was to be the infotainment for the evening. I was busy marketing, so I didn't get a chance to play, and just as well since my handicap is like forty.

The senior regional sales leader at Merrill, who was a member of the course, had rented out the entire club. We had the place to ourselves. I arrived just as the golf rounds ended and the festivities began: champagne and sensational hors d'oeuvres to start, followed by a four-course meal by a Michelin-starred chef, and access to the high-end wine cellar. The evening ended with copious amounts of cognac and scotch. It was a first-rate evening, and all I had to do was show up, speak for about thirty minutes, keep it light and humorous, and make sure I began before my third glass of wine. Good thing my part started on the early side of the evening because the bottles of 1985 Chateau Lafite were beckoning.

On the edge of the golf course were guest houses where the Merrill sales force put its clients up for the night. As for me, I was marketing for the equity team the next day and had to have that car drive me back to my hotel in downtown Atlanta. I was never too concerned about performing with a hangover because I always made sure I had the cure with me: Alka Seltzer. As far as I'm concerned, it is a cure for everything. I knew I had a crazy day ahead of me because Sloan Luckie, one of the sales guys on the Southeast equity team, was driving me to Birmingham, Alabama, for a day of client meetings. We were driving instead of flying to save money (and because Sloan, a terrific guy, wasn't fond of air travel). I can't recall the model, but it was a small, older vehicle. Might have been a 1995 Honda Civic. Thank goodness the A/C was working. It was a three-hour drive.

There is so much history in the Deep South that it was actually a very interesting drive. The route we were taking passed many Civil War battlefields. Sloan, who is African American, was like a tour guide, pointing out all the various sites along the way. It was one trip I have never forgotten.

We reached the outskirts of Birmingham and Sloan stopped in a parking lot at a strip mall. I thought he was stopping to take a break, and I got out to stretch my legs and answer some emails on my Blackberry. Sloan was already on the sidewalk of the outdoor plaza. He yelled at me, "Rosie, what the hell are you doing? The clients are already here for our breakfast meeting!"

What?

Breakfast was in a diner. A classic greasy spoon, right out of the *Alice* sitcom from the mid-1970s, with red and white checkered tablecloths and bar stools by the counter. I was the only one in a suit and tie. I should have taken Sloan's lead and left my jacket and tie in the car. You should have seen the stares I got. It reminded me of Michael J. Fox in *Back to the Future* when he first goes into the 1950s and everyone is fixated on his orange puffer vest layered over his denim jacket. The folks at this diner looked at me as though I was from outer space. They weren't accustomed to seeing Armani suits at that establishment.

There were already six clients sitting at a table. We sat down, ordered our grits, eggs, hash browns, sausages, and toast, and I began the discussion with words that were not particularly bullish for the equity market. You see, this was early 2003, and the bond market had been on fire for three years as the tech wreck lingered and dragged the equity market into a bear phase for the same length of time. I was still bullish on fixed-income and cautious on the stock market. You could say I was still loaded for bear at the time, even as the stock market and Treasury yields were both forming a bottom.

I recall a trucker who looked just like Paul Bunyan sitting beside our table. It looked to me as though he was jotting down some notes as I spoke. Later on, after I realized that I was on the wrong side of the trade and had overstayed my welcome on the long bond/short equity theme, I had nightmares that this guy would find a way to track me down and chop me to pieces.

The bill came at the end of the breakfast, and I think the whole thing came to $80 with the tip. For eight of us. As we got back in the car, I said, "Sloan, what was that all about? Last night, the fixed-income team throws a $10,000 gala for its clients at a flashy golf course, and here you spend $80 on a client breakfast."

"Rosie," he said, "that was the bond team last night, and their marketing budget is huge. I represent the equity team, and our budget is next to nil."

Being a classic contrarian, I am ashamed to say I missed that signal. One asset class was getting all the attention, money, and marketing. The other was being ignored. That was exactly when the tide began to turn against the Treasury market and for the equity market. It was times like this that Bob Farrell was talking about when he advised that if everyone was on one side, the trade was over. But I was caught flatfooted. It happens. When

I recounted this story months later to my pal and Merrill chief equity strategist, Richard Bernstein, he said to me, "I wish you would have called in that story to me the day it happened."

The big lesson here: always check your blind spots.

CHAPTER 21

Calling a Bubble a Mania

While writing this book, I was interviewed on CNBC and told that my views were diametrically opposed to the current bullish consensus and market positioning. I exclaimed that it had been many years since I was this excited about going against the herd. I managed to work in Bob Farrell's Rule #9: "When all the experts and forecasts agree, something else is going to happen." The whole discussion was really about whether the economy and inflation were getting out of control—and what that meant for interest rates, the Federal Reserve's actions, and the bond market. I'm happy to say I didn't take the bait on the stock market—the bubble was just getting bigger and bigger, with the smoothed CAPE market multiple now pressing against forty times, a level historically surpassed only by the late 1990s tech frenzy.

So, no, I am not positioned the way the dominant "Roaring Twenties" crowd is today. I have been outside the consensus before. When I turned bearish on tech at the height of the bubble in 2000, my partners at the time thought I was nuts. Same thing in early 2002, when the bond vigilantes were out in force. They had visions of inflation spiking due to post-9/11 reconstruction and rebuilding, alongside massive monetary and fiscal stimulus, and were selling bonds aggressively. I disagreed. The economy was far too fragile to withstand the run-up in market rates, though this wasn't evident to the consensus at the time. A classic inventory investment cycle appeared to be taking hold prematurely. Alan Greenspan signaled to the market in early 2002 that it was over its skis on the big economic recovery view—but, as is the case now, investors guffawed. The second half of that year saw a monster Treasury market rally as expectations of Fed tightening swung around to easing. The consensus gasped.

I can't say I get every call right—who does?—but that counter-consensus call on the Fed held me in good stead as I was making my trek to New York. I needed that boost, because my resolve was truly tested during that mania in the mid-2000s.

All I had to do was sift through the data and see the charts to know we had a housing bubble of epic proportions on our hands. Home price-to-income, home price-to-rent, and residential real estate/household asset ratios were in the stratosphere. When you're talking about one-to-two standard deviation events, you know you are in major excess.

Nevertheless, I was under intense pressure from Merrill's senior management in 2007 to do two things: stop calling for Fed rate cuts; and stop using the term "bubble" to describe the US housing market in my published research. This was arguably the most disappointing and stressful period of my tenure at Merrill Lynch. I peeved off so many people by not joining the bullish consensus. I faced multiple internal reviews and years of internal disdain for my position.

Let's tackle the first point here: the Fed. This was all happening around the time of the peak in all risk-on trades. We were coming off a two-year Fed tightening cycle (2004–2006) that took the funds rate up from a low of 1 percent to a peak of 5.25 percent. Rate hikes, under Fed chairman Ben Bernanke, stopped in the summer of 2006. Knowing from historical precedent that the Fed typically cuts rates after holding steady for a year or more following a tightening cycle, I subtly incorporated a series of rate cuts into my forecast starting in 2008 to signal my inclination to clients. Although the stock market didn't definitively peak until October 9, 2007, I observed the S&P 500 forming a topping pattern. Concurrently, the boom in China was driving industrial commodity and oil prices sharply higher. I suspected this was another bubble poised to burst. I pushed back against the view that rates were going higher, and hard as it might be to believe in retrospect, it required daring to not join the crowd calling for a tighter Fed and an extended bear market in Treasuries.

My call for rate cuts was undoubtedly controversial. To my knowledge, no one else on Wall Street was predicting Fed easing. A year prior, I had been appointed chair of Merrill's Interest Rate Committee. The committee comprised members of fixed-income research, analysts, and strategists from other divisions. Senior management had become frustrated with me because I was perceived as a "policy dove" and had consistently lagged behind the Fed throughout the tightening cycle from 2004 to 2006. I was significantly behind the curve and missed most of that two-year cyclical bear market in bonds. As a consequence of being wrong for so long, I was stripped of the sole responsibility for the Fed view, and it was now subject to a committee vote, albeit one that I chaired—management at least gave me the lead role!

That was hardly the worst that happened to me in this period. One particular event that resonates to this day was a phone call I received from Richard Klein in the autumn of 2005. Richard was head of equity sales out of London and a great friend and supporter.

"Rosie, I need you to tell me quickly what your top ten most accurate calls have been so far this year."

"Oh, that's easy," I said, and quickly rhymed off three. Four and five were a stretch, mind you, and I really struggled after that. Why couldn't he have just asked me for the "top three?"

I asked what this was all about and he told me in confidence that the global heads were meeting up at headquarters in New York that Monday to discuss one thing. My fate. And he needed ammunition to ward off my executioners.

I recall being in synagogue the day after I got back to Toronto (a little praying in the forecasting business can never hurt) and I recall one of the congregants, who was a senior financial guy on Bay Street, whispered in my ear, "I hear you're about to get fired." Good Lord, but does word travel fast. Rumors and innuendo know no borders.

I do remember praying extra hard that particular Saturday. It must have worked because as I waited for the axe to fall that following week, I never got any call from anyone. A while later, I asked Richard what had happened and he told me that while my supporters were outnumbered at that meeting, they were more influential and powerful and so their opinions carried the day. But he did make a point of telling me that it wouldn't hurt to start dialing down my bearish view on the economy and equity market and go easy on the extremely unpopular housing-bubble narrative. Sure thing. Go easy on the what turned out to be the biggest and most successful call of my entire career.

I can't say that I didn't give a damn about having Damocles's sword over my head all that time at Merrill Lynch. But at some point, I practically became immune to the pressure. I survived because my calls had nothing to do with my work ethic, and that included being there 24/7 for the client base, which is why even in those years in the wilderness over my crazy early call on the bubble and the burst, I was constantly ranked near the top of the institutional investor surveys. Whether you are right or wrong, there is no substitute for always being present, diligent, always willing to leave it all out there, and be interesting just enough to fill a room even when the masses believe you're from outer space. Thing is, easier said than done for most economists who prefer to hug the consensus and stay out of trouble with senior management. Going against the herd involves taking risks but anyone in my business should never make their masters happy when it means putting clients in harm's way.

Shortly before the collapse began in the summer-fall of 2007, I received a call from senior management encouraging me to reconsider the forecast and change it from rate cuts to rate hikes. In the "sell side" of the business, predicting rate cuts implies underlying economic problems, so forecasting interest rate reductions is generally avoided. As I often say, everyone in this business seems to believe in fairy tales—they're always talking about a Goldilocks market. I recall being told by one of my superiors that the equity research analysts were complaining that if they were to input my economics department's forecasts on retail sales, industrial production, and housing starts into their own models, they would be forced to have "sell" recommendations on 75 percent of the companies they covered. To which I responded, "Maybe they should." That didn't engender a warm response.

Other senior leaders at Merrill research were advocating for rate hikes, even if that wasn't the committee's consensus, and my manager made a point of informing me of that. I asked if I was being relieved of the responsibility of calling the Fed. I was simply instructed to propose the possibility of rate hikes to the committee for a vote at our next meeting, which I did. However, in my introduction to the group, I stated that while I could be persuaded to remove the forecast of rate cuts in 2008, I would resign from the committee if the vote indicated the Fed would tighten. Ultimately, we voted to eliminate the cuts and maintain the funds rate at 5.25 percent, where it had been for over a year. I was unhappy about it, but my hands were tied.

A few weeks later, two of Bear Stearns' subprime MBS hedge funds collapsed and declared bankruptcy. In mid-August, the Fed cut the discount rate by 50 basis points, and I immediately called an emergency committee meeting. I made it clear that all the work my economics team and I had done for the past year had proven prescient, highlighting the underlying economic fragility that no one wanted to acknowledge. I insisted that we quickly vote to reinstate our rate-cut call and add even more cuts to our original forecast, as this was no longer a superficial adjustment.

One committee member argued that reversing course so quickly would make us appear indecisive. I responded, "I don't care. It will be obvious to everyone that we were pressured to make the initial change, and I believe our clients will ultimately appreciate our prompt pivot. This marks the beginning of the credit collapse we had been anticipating, and there is no time to lose." I don't remember the exact number of rate cuts we included in this revised forecast, but considering the Fed eventually cut rates by 500 basis points to the zero bound by early 2009, I'm certain it wasn't sufficient. The fact that I was being encouraged to call for hikes is astounding.

* * *

Regarding the second point of pressure from senior management, a year before those hedge funds failed, they advised me to stop using the word "bubble" in my work. That is absolutely true. There was leverage, speculation, valuation, sentiment, and public participation—all the telltale signals of a bubble. But I was instructed to avoid the word. I was told the term was too emotional, that it was upsetting and frightening people at Merrill, and that I needed to find a new way to describe the situation.

Imagine being forbidden from using the term "bubble" in published research even as we headed into the peak of one of the most severe housing and credit market bubbles in history! When I asked if I could replace "bubble" with the word "mania," I was told that would be acceptable. There wasn't a significant difference between the words, but something about the word "bubble" put everyone on edge. You can't make this stuff up.

The issue wasn't confined to internal politics at Merrill Lynch. On October 9, 2007, I visited the Fed in Washington, DC, prepared to deliver a forceful presentation outlining why a recession was imminent. My presentation was met with general derision. As I waited outside the Fed building for my car to take me to the airport, one of the senior Fed officials from the meeting said to me, "You know, Rosenberg, the S&P 500 just closed at a record high." Indeed, it had, at 1,565. The index wouldn't reach that level again until March 28, 2013, almost six years later. And the recession that no one saw coming began in December of that year, just two months after I was essentially laughed out of the Fed's ornate boardroom.

Then there were the clients. Around that time, I was on a marketing tour of Houston. I visited a very large mutual fund. During one of my usual "fire and brimstone" presentations, armed with charts demonstrating the impending housing market collapse and arguing that the long bond was the only worthwhile investment, the chief investment officer stood up, interrupted me, and shouted, "Rosenberg, I've heard enough; you don't know what you're talking about!" Ouch. There were a number of other comments that aren't suitable to print. I immediately thought, "Well, that's one institutional investor I've lost."

In fairness to the chief investment officer, the head of bond sales at my own firm did exactly the same thing, except he physically threw my chart package at me in front of about thirty people. I thought I was supposed to be giving the "pitch." I'll never forget what he said: "Do you enjoy being wrong all the time?" Of course, when push came to shove, I proved to be spectacularly correct, and he didn't last much longer at the firm.

Look, nobody is right all the time, and nobody is wrong all the time. More often than not, it really comes down to timing, and I am historically early to a fault. But experience goes a long way in this business. Not succumbing to that pressure to forecast a Fed rate hike is one of my proudest moments in my thirty-five years in this business. And it's important to identify bubbles, even if you're early. We have two now, in residential real estate and equities. It's equally important to understand that excesses will always go further than you think, which we're now seeing, and to remember that no bubble ever corrected by going sideways. There's no sense trying to time it. Just know that it's out there.

We're in another era of consensus, much like 2000, 2002, and 2007. We are said to have sticky inflation, everyone has bearish views on the Treasury market, and there is rampant bullishness on the AI trade and equity markets. This consensus is so overwhelmingly one-sided that I never find it difficult to find people who will take me in the other direction. The pushback against my contrary view received from the general investing public is incredible, but it is actually increasing the intensity of my resolve. As Bob Farrell would surely posit, "something else is going to happen."

CHAPTER 22

The Thing About CEOs

I recall the first time Stan O'Neal, Merrill's chief executive officer, called me into his office. It was shortly after he became CEO and I became chief economist, sometime in early 2003. Sitting across from him at his desk, I was totally petrified. During our conversation, I accidentally spilled coffee cream on his desk. I frantically got up to clean up the mess. Stan said, "Don't worry about it." I sheepishly responded, "Stan, anyone who spills cream on a Fortune 500 CEO's desk should be plenty worried." He laughed, and I look back at that moment as having broken the ice.

Stan had a reputation as a brutal leader who fired many senior people, including some instrumental in the firm's success. Jeff Kronthal comes to mind—a true Wall Street Legend who was in the top six rungs of management and was largely responsible for the years of success Merrill enjoyed under his leadership. I heard many horror stories about how he treated his senior staff. Regardless, we got along fine. He was always courteous and friendly to me. He even had me fill in for him at a client event in Palm Springs sometime in 2005, flying me solo in his private jet. Too bad I had to speak that evening, or I would have raided the bar, replete with top-notch single malt.

I doubt Stan would have given the same sermon I delivered that evening, typically focusing on tail risks and what life will look like after the bubble burst, because all bubbles burst. In fact, I know he wouldn't have delivered a similar message, because I later found out that Stan O'Neal, Merrill's CEO and my ultimate boss, was betting against my views.

A good friend and former colleague recently reminded me of the Tuesday "risk meetings" led by Dow Kim, the Merrill executive in charge of the entire fixed-income operation. I always got along well with Dow, as I did with Stan, but as the credit bubble peaked, Stan essentially gave Dow free rein—this has been well documented. I attended those meetings in the mid-2000s with Richard Bernstein and all the fixed-income heads. If I remember correctly, Dow would always ask if the desks were taking on enough risk. When they said they could take more, he told them to do so. When they later said they were adequately positioned, he told them to take on more risk. And when they said they were taking on too much risk, Dow fired them. There is plenty of blame to go around regarding Merrill Lynch's demise, and it wasn't just Stan O'Neal's fault.

It was around this same time that a famous Wall Street hedge fund manager—I can't tell you his name because I agreed to keep his confidence—offered me a job. He followed my work closely and acted upon and profited from my research. We became good friends over time. His pitch went like this: "Why do you want to work at a bank that doesn't listen to you? Come work for me—because I do listen to you."

I asked for clarification. He told me that Merrill Lynch CEO, Stan O'Neal, was in his office, sitting in the same seat as I was, and as they were getting set to make a mortgage trade, Stan was on the long side, and the manager I am referring to was on the short side. (Guess who came out on top?) This information sent a chill down my spine. I wondered what Stan had been thinking all those times when I was presenting my views to him in his office? Probably laughing inside.

One of my favorite memories of Stan O'Neal was an experience at the Merrill gym in the middle of the afternoon. I was on the treadmill when he walked in and saw me. I thought he was going to ask, "Why aren't you at the desk?" Instead, he patted me on the back and said, "I'm glad to see you're working on your health." At that point, I had become so sedentary that I had ballooned to 240 pounds. I'm only 5 feet, 8 inches tall! After finishing my workout and showering, I was in the locker room getting ready to leave when I saw Stan, with a bath towel around his waist. He started to banter with me. The conversation turned into a discussion about the day's data, what the Fed was likely to do, the market reaction, and so on. This was maybe the closest we ever came to a debate. Before I knew it, a circle of about twelve guys had formed around us to watch. It was like being at a schoolyard fight, with the other students trying to get the best view. But as it always was with me and Stan, it was just a courteous exchange of views. I think the onlookers were disappointed that it wasn't more than that, but I knew better than to undress a CEO, even if he was only wearing a towel.

* * *

While Stan O'Neal initiated Merrill Lynch's downfall by surrounding himself with fixed-income "experts"—cold-blooded individuals who loved leverage—they lacked a fundamental understanding of counterparty risk and the complex structured debt products they were buying. When O'Neal finally recognized the looming crisis, he attempted to extricate the firm from these malinvestments. He even met with executives at another bank to explore a merger or capital infusion in an attempt to save Merrill. He was dismissed in October 2007, almost a year before the worst of the crisis hit, for having failed to secure appropriate board approvals beforehand. Despite his firing, the reason was not what most people assume, and Merrill still had time to recover.

I believe the real demise of Merrill occurred under John Thain, the former president and co-COO of Goldman Sachs, who replaced O'Neal and brought several of his Goldman lieutenants with him. In early 2008, I was repeatedly asked if Merrill should conduct a series of capital raises, and I consistently advocated for "as many as possible." In the wake of the Bear Stearns debacle, the markets had temporarily stabilized. However, the small window of opportunity we had was lost when John Thain, as I was told, deemed it "too expensive." It seems the new senior management failed to recognize that no price was too high to save this pioneering ninety-three-year-old firm.

By this time, I was merely a figurehead at Merrill Lynch. Stan never heeded my recommendations to de-risk; this reality became particularly clear during an experience in early 2009.

I was invited to a last-minute meeting in the Merrill executive boardroom to address a billionaire family client from Michigan. I was told it was "super important," forcing me to reschedule my day, which was supposed to be spent marketing in Midtown for the equity sales desk. This meeting took place in late 2008, shortly after the Lehman and AIG collapse and Bank of America's buyout of Merrill Lynch.

I had printed several chart packages, expecting to deliver a macro/market presentation. Upon arriving in the boardroom, I found members of the family, including the regal patriarch, their family office representative, two Merrill financial advisors (both of whom, I suspect, were later laid off), and their boss.

As I distributed the presentation packages, the patriarch stated, "Mr. Rosenberg, we did not ask you to attend this meeting to hear your market views. We are already familiar with your views, so there is no need."

"Okay. So why am I here?"

"I'll tell you why. I wanted to have the opportunity to ask you in person why your own firm doesn't listen to you."

Uh oh. I could see those two advisors starting to slide under the table.

"I'm not sure I follow you," I said.

He then spent ten minutes explaining that his family had suffered significant losses by being concentrated in Merrill's highest risk investments.

It was only recently that the family had discovered that Merrill Lynch had a chief economist who had predicted the crisis. Early, perhaps, but it's always better to be early than late when a bear market begins. Bull markets are escalators that go up, while bear markets are elevators that plunge down.

As it turned out, these two advisors had ensured that this billionaire family never received my research. They were purposefully kept in the dark about my assessment of the landscape. The patriarch held a report I had published a year prior, in the autumn of 2007. "Why was I never sent this?" he bellowed.

The walls of the boardroom shook. A few moments of silence followed. The two advisors were practically hiding under the table at this point.

As I was packing my things to leave, guess who walked into the room?

John Thain.

The patriarch said to me, "Mr. Rosenberg, please stay a little while longer." I texted Francine, my sensational assistant, to let the institutional sales desk know my whole afternoon was now up in the air.

The patriarch was polite to the CEO. "Hi John, nice to see you again. Come around the table, I want you to meet my family." Everyone stood up, John shook hands with the family members, and as he approached me, he extended his hand and said, "Nice to meet you as well."

"John," retorted the patriarch. "Mr. Rosenberg is not part of the family. Surely you know your own chief economist."

Awkward! The fact of the matter is that we had never met. I had only met John's senior advisors who had followed him from Goldman. When John joined Merrill as CEO in December 2007, I emailed him a thoughtful welcoming note, offering my team's and my services in any capacity, especially given that the financial crisis was just gaining momentum. I never received a response. When I mentioned this to some of his senior advisors sometime later, they expressed surprise.

Anyway, I could see the shock on John's face after the patriarch's comment. I tried to look away so I wouldn't be caught laughing, but John quickly recovered, saying as he kept shaking my hand, "Of course I know, Dave. How are you, Dave?" He patted me on the back. Sure thing.

We all sat back down around the board table and the patriarch turned to John, who was sitting at the head of the table. I was at the other end. "John," he said, "I'm going to ask you the same thing I asked Mr. Rosenberg." He never addressed me by my first name. "Why does a firm like yours employ a chief economist that it doesn't listen to?"

If I began to squirm, I could only imagine what was going on in John's head.

"I read Dave every day," said John, "and I know full well what he is saying. The entire management team listens to him."

With that, I really had to leave. My entire afternoon and evening had been rearranged for this meeting, and I had a car waiting outside to drive me to midtown for my client engagements. As I exited, the person who I believe was responsible for the family office of the patriarch and his siblings and offspring followed me to the elevator.

"Mr. Rosenberg," he asked, "can we be put on the mailing list for your research material going forward?"

"Absolutely," I said. "And only my kids call me Mr. Rosenberg. You can call me Dave."

But wait, there's more. Later that afternoon, while I was between meetings, Francine called me on my cell to say, "I had to rearrange your day tomorrow, too."

"Good grief, what happened this time?"

"John Thain's assistant just called, and he wants you to have lunch with him in his office tomorrow."

So, we had lunch. Whatever we talked about, we never once touched on the economy or the markets. Pure small talk. But, hey, now he could honestly say that he'd met me.

* * *

By January or February of 2009, I knew it was time to return to Toronto. I was on the "bubble," certain that I was going to resign soon. The hedge fund desk at Merrill took me out for steak and wine with the senior people at a famous (now defunct) hedge fund, Galleon. After we went to a New York Rangers game at Madison Square Garden, I sat next to Angela Dalton, who was the co-head of investments at the fund and a valued client.

Not long after the puck dropped, she pulled a report from her bag. "Does this look familiar?"

"Yeah, that's my report from this morning," I replied.

"Do you remember what you said?"

"I'm thinking more about what I'm going to pen tomorrow."

She then showed me that morning's Morning Market Memo, covered in writing, including arrows pointing up and down. "Do you know we meet every morning just to discuss your daily?"

I was shocked.

"It's true," she continued. "Now, you may not recall what you wrote today, but you pushed us out of one trade and into two new positions. You're a savant."

I am not making any of this up! She pointed to the two Merrill sales guys and said, out of earshot, "I bet they never told you the commissions we paid them today based on what you had to say." Of course, they didn't!

Angela then revealed that she wasn't really a hockey fan and suggested we ditch the game for drinks and a chat. During that conversation, she asked, "Why on earth don't you start your own research consulting firm?"

I wasn't at liberty to tell her I was on the verge of announcing my departure from Merrill, and frankly, I wasn't sure what my next gig would be. But I was intrigued by her idea. Angela asked the server for a sheet of paper and mapped out the entire strategy for me to start my own firm. It would take eleven years to turn it into a reality, but I owe Angela Dalton a huge debt of gratitude.

CHAPTER 23

Finding My Way Home

At the beginning of 2009, I had just been ranked second in the *Institutional Investor* vote for Wall Street economists. Nobody was ever going to knock Ed Hyman off his lofty perch (he placed first forty-four times). I had also just come off making the most successful call of my career: predicting the bursting of the housing and credit market bubble, although the fallout turned out to be far worse than I could have imagined. Suddenly, all my prior detractors were my best friends, a testament to the fickle nature of the forecasting business. Furthermore, I had made the cut at the new Bank of America-Merrill Lynch merger, which was actually more of a takeover. After BoA bought Merrill to save it in 2008, the decision-makers had to choose who would stay and who would go. There was a lot of redundancy across sales, trading, investment banking, and research. My rival was the widely respected Micky Levy, the chief economist at BoA, but he ended up being promoted to an advisory role for Ken Lewis, the CEO at the time (the last job I would have wanted). My team also expanded, absorbing some of Micky's staff.

Nevertheless, I was at a crossroads. Merrill wasn't Merrill anymore. While its excellent culture had been eroded during the Stan O'Neal era, it was still fundamentally great. Despite the pressures to change my views, the fact that I survived as a bear for so long at a firm where a bull was the logo—right there on everyone's business cards—attests to the corporate tolerance and support for differentiated views, at least within some important circles of the bank. I believe the people in charge knew all along that despite my not being a catalyst to pitch risky products, I was always there for the client base. What else matters in the end?

Throughout the BoA transition, in late 2008 and early 2009, my staff would come into my office and ask if their jobs were safe. I told them the truth: I had no clue. I didn't even know whether Micky or I would make the cut in the newly merged firm. It was a period of heightened uncertainty in the markets, the economy, and, on a personal level for me and my team. All I could tell people was that, despite the turmoil and anxiety, the best way to maximize our odds of survival was to continue producing thought-provoking and innovative research, staying in close touch with the sales force and our clients, and remaining focused rather than wallowing in self-pity or getting consumed by fear.

I don't want to downplay the fear at the time. Again, I started in this business in October 1987 on the day the S&P 500 plunged 23 percent in one session, the worst since the Great Crash of 1929. But the 1987 collapse was brief. It came and went. The Fed only had to cut rates three times to set off a rally by early 1988. This time, we faced not only plummeting markets but global systemic risk and severe counterparty risk with a total lack of trust between market participants—who was hiding worthless assets on their balance sheets and what were the exposures to everyone else?

By the time the Great Financial Crisis of 2008 accelerated in September, the Fed had not only cut rates nearly to zero but also embarked on a range of interventionist measures with acronyms galore, from TAF to TSLF to PDCF to CPFF to AMLF to TALF. The stock market would surge each time the Fed publicly announced one of these. After each intervention, I was asked whether the crisis had passed. It was like children on a road trip—"are we there yet?" We weren't. The Fed's mistake, at least until TARP in early 2009—which required the Treasury's involvement in recapitalizing the banks with Congressional approval—was thinking for months that we had a liquidity crisis when we actually had an insolvency crisis that risked bringing down the entire global financial system.

All this reminded me of when the Greenspan-led Fed in 2000 thought we were experiencing an inventory correction instead of a detonation of the technology capital stock. That realization prompted the central bank to cut rates by 50 basis points outside of its scheduled meetings on the first trading day of 2001. But it wasn't enough to prevent the tech-wreck recession from taking hold in March—a recession that the consensus economics community totally missed, as is typical.

I recall walking in midtown Manhattan in December 2008 and stopping at the corner of 34th Street and Broadway, right in front of Macy's. I looked at the Salvation Army Santa ringing his bell. I looked him right in the eyes and saw that he was catatonic, as was everyone at that time. It was pure fear, the likes of which I had never witnessed before or since, and my career had already spanned not only October 1987 but two Iraq wars, 9/11, the Asian crisis, and destabilizing fallout from the Long-Term Capital Management fiasco, the tech wreck, and, in Canada, the near-demise of our country with the Quebec vote on separation in 1995.

In early 2009, as the Great Financial Crisis reached its lowest point, I was spent. Seven years of living out of a suitcase more than half the time, managing up and down, and dodging constant backstabbing had taken its toll. My family life was falling apart, making my lifestyle unsustainable. Even if I had wanted to continue flying back and forth between New York and Toronto, the stress of it all would have killed me. The truth was, I missed my family dearly and needed to find balance and stability. Having accomplished everything I set out to do since taking the job in late 2002, and having scored that number-two ranking, I could leave at the top of my game with my head held high.

So, in early 2009, I discreetly put feelers out on Bay Street. Several big banks expressed interest, including my two former employers, Bank of

Nova Scotia and Bank of Montreal (TD Bank had also expressed interest). At Scotia, Warren was retiring and encouraged senior management to consider me as his successor. At BMO, the legendary Don Coxe had retired, and the leadership thought I would be an adequate replacement. Other offers came in, as well. But then Gluskin Sheff entered the fray, and that changed everything. They weren't a big bank, but a boutique wealth manager based in Toronto.

It so happened that during a marketing trip to Toronto in January 2009, I had stopped by Gluskin Sheff's offices. I typically saw this group three or four times a year, and I considered them to be among the brightest fund managers on Bay Street. They had a first-rate reputation. I gave my usual impassioned presentation, and the next day, they bought a table right at the front of the room for my broader client lunch presentation.

A day or two after my marketing schedule in Toronto wrapped up, I flew back to New York City and received an email from Ira Gluskin, the co-founder. I had known Ira for decades but had never received an email from him before. In fact, I was pretty sure he didn't know how to use email. I'd heard that his assistant, Patricia, handled that for him. But it was an incredibly gracious email, thanking me for coming in to address the team and adding that he had reviewed my reports from the previous year and was struck by how I had stuck to my guns and, in the end, had been proven prescient. He added that I should consider returning to Toronto at some point—he couldn't have known that the wheels were already in motion. I fired back an email saying something to the effect that the next time I presented to Gluskin Sheff, I would be tempted to attach my CV to my chart package.

Patricia had printed out my email response for Ira, who took it to the office of Bill Webb. At that time, Bill was taking over the position of chief investment officer from Ira. "I think Rosenberg may be in play," said Ira, handing Bill the email. "You may want to chat with him, but it's your call in the end."

* * *

I knew many of the key players at Gluskin Sheff, and none better than Bill, who sadly succumbed to cancer in the autumn of 2023. I'd first come across Bill when he was a young analyst on one of the Gluskin Sheff funds and marveled at how he successfully climbed the firm's ladder. He was an amazing person. We had deep admiration for one another, both before and after I joined the company. I don't have a lot of good things to say about all the senior people at my former firm, but Bill was a mensch and one of the few you could trust and lean on. Excellent emotional intelligence. I miss him to this day.

Bill called to tell me that Ira had shown him the email I'd sent, and that he'd jump at a chance to talk. So we met at a Starbucks in downtown Toronto the following week. I discreetly told him about my situation, not wanting word to get back to Merrill Lynch that I was considering a departure. Then again, as I told him, it wasn't really Merrill Lynch anymore—it was Bank of America, headquartered in Charlotte. Nothing against Charlotte, but it's not Manhattan. My manners suited Manhattan. I remember a client dinner in the Midwest when I let loose a few expletives aimed mostly at the Federal Reserve. The BoA salesperson sitting to my right whispered in my ear, "Dave, this isn't New York."

It was always like that with BoA. After the merger, I was flying to Charlotte every two weeks to meet my new masters. Whereas Merrill had been filled with mavericks, shooting from the hip most of the time, BoA was as buttoned-down as could be, formal beyond formal. I recall one visit to Charlotte when we took some BoA clients out for lunch. As I reached for a bread roll after we sat down, the sales guy, who I had just met, kicked me under the table and shook his head. Then one of the clients bowed his head and said, "Let us say grace." I felt more at home at the diner in Birmingham. I was the only one to order a glass of wine.

Anyway, the coffee with Bill went really well. He suggested a lunch the following week with the senior partners at Gluskin Sheff, and said I shouldn't be surprised if they made me an offer. That lunch meeting in their ornate boardroom went great. The only uncomfortable moment came when Ira asked if I was a good golfer, not even bothering to ask if I golfed at all. It was just assumed. He said a ton of business was conducted on the links in the spring and summer. I could attest to that; in my eleven years at the firm, between May and September, no one at a senior level was ever in the office on Fridays.

"It depends what you mean by 'good,'" I told Ira.

"Okay, what's your typical score?"

I felt a lump in my throat—did the offer hinge on my handicap?

"I don't know, like 120."

"Oh, so you don't really golf."

"Jeez, Ira, I wasn't even counting mulligans."

That line killed. As the senior folks at Gluskin Sheff discovered over the years, nobody did the nineteenth tee better than me. That's how they used me at the club once the client game was over.

I didn't immediately accept the Gluskin Sheff offer because I had a growing list of other banks vying for my attention. Ultimately, the Bank of Nova Scotia presented the most appealing contract. I was upfront with Bill and told him about the competing offers I was considering.

About a month after our initial coffee, I was back in Toronto for another speaking engagement. Bill, at the time, hosted a weekly BNN television show with business reporter Howard Green. According to Bill, Howard suggested bringing on a guest. Bill immediately thought of me. Howard asked, "Isn't Dave in New York?" Bill replied, "I know for a fact that he is in Toronto today, and I'll see if he'll come on the show with us." So Bill called. The show ran from 5:00 p.m. to 6:00 p.m., and I was available. I accepted.

The hour-long show was phenomenal. Bill and I were like Lennon and McCartney. Our karma was incredible. We fed off each other's energy. After the show, Howard declared it arguably the best he had ever hosted. I felt great. I accepted Bill's offer for a ride home. I don't know why, since my car was near the studio, but what the heck? I'd pick it up tomorrow morning. Some gravitational pull took me into Bill's SUV and we continued our discussion—not about my employment opportunity, but extending our talk on BNN about macroeconomics and markets. It was a constant flow of back-and-forth views, and I was jazzed.

When we arrived at my house and were in the driveway, I turned to Bill and said, "I have something I want to tell you. After this show with Howard Green and the half hour in the car with you, I can't help but feel this burst of energy. I'm going to block out all the other offers in front of me right now and focus only on yours."

Bill unbuckled his seat belt, leaned over, and gave me a giant hug. Bill was a very big man, and I feared that he would crush me before I ever had a chance to sign on the dotted line. It also crossed my mind that the neighbors might be watching and get the wrong idea.

When I walked through the front door, Rachael was waiting for me in the hallway. She said that she and the kids had watched me and Bill on the BNN show and that "this was the best I have ever seen you on TV." I told Rachael what I had said to Bill in his truck, and all I can remember is her draping her arms around my neck. Through all the ups and downs of working at Gluskin Sheff—especially after the founders, Ira and Gerry, had cashed in their chips—it turned out to be a great decision for me and my family.

The problem with going to a major Canadian bank was that I would have faced the same challenges I had at Merrill—not just navigating a huge bureaucracy with multiple reporting lines, but tons of travel. I needed to limit the amount of time I was going to be away from home, and the fact that Gluskin Sheff clients were mostly located in Toronto, Montreal, and Vancouver was fine with me.

* * *

Although I hadn't yet resigned from Merrill Lynch (BoA), I had drafted a resignation letter. I was prepared to hand it to Candace Browning, head of global research and my longtime manager. I asked my executive assistant, Francine, to schedule a meeting with Candace in her office within the next few days.

Shortly after, I received an invitation for a breakfast meeting at the Four Seasons with Candace and Adam Quinton, her number two at the time and the newly appointed head of research for the Americas. I questioned Francine, "I thought I asked for a meeting alone with Candace in her office." Francine replied, "This invite came in just as I was about to arrange that." Weird.

In any event, the three of us met for breakfast at the Four Seasons, either in February or March of 2009. I had my resignation letter tucked inside my suit jacket pocket, ready to drop the bomb. But Candace immediately said, "I bet you're wondering why we are here."

"Yes."

"This is a celebration."

"Of what?"

"You know that Rich Bernstein is stepping aside, right?"

Rich and I were good friends, and we were both aware of each other's situations; we even discussed starting our own firm together at one point. I shrugged and said, "I know he wants to start running money independently."

"That is correct, and we are going to help him." Then, she dropped her own bomb. "We are celebrating because we are promoting you to chief economist and strategist. We know you had this title back in Toronto, but you will be the first to have the dual role on Wall Street." This unexpected offer came with significantly more money, staff, resources, and responsibility.

I left my resignation letter in my pocket. Candace and Adam were smiling, chatting, and enjoying the moment, discussing this amazing opportunity. She had secured buy-in from all the top executives at the newly merged bank. As for me? I was in a trance, barely able to concentrate. I was in a complete daze. I had come to the breakfast meeting prepared to resign. I had undergone intense mental preparation for my resignation, knowing that Candace would not take the news well, especially with Rich leaving the firm around the same time. I didn't say much during the breakfast, just asked a few questions. My heart was racing faster than when I'd first arrived at the restaurant.

What should I do? This was the career opportunity of a lifetime. Should I accept it? Or risk irreparably damaging my family life?

Then an image flashed into my head: the crucial pipe-smoking scene in Roman Polanski's 1968 thriller, *Rosemary's Baby*, the moment Guy Woodhouse sells his soul to the devil. I'm a bit of a movie buff, and that scene perfectly captured my dilemma. If you haven't seen the movie, I won't spoil it. It's a classic, as creepy and spine-tingling as a film can be. The check came to the table and Candace picked it up. As she and Adam got up to leave, I stopped them.

"Candace," I said, "there's something I have to tell you."

I handed her my resignation letter, thanking her profusely for her support and for the amazing offer. But I had been away from my family for the better part of seven years, and it was time for me to come home. We ended up sitting at the table for another hour, trying to find a solution, including the possibility of me working full-time out of Toronto in this new and expanded role. I appreciated the gesture but also realized that to be successful in this job, I needed to be in New York. I wasn't going to set myself up for failure for any amount of money. Besides, I knew it wouldn't be long before my life at airports and endless flight delays, on my way to all four corners of the world, would resume.

Candace returned with an even more lucrative offer. But when I discussed these counteroffers with Rachael and the boys and saw the utter despondency on their faces, I felt my heart sink. It brought back memories of Jacob's guttural sighs on Sunday nights when I told him I was going back to New York for the week.

So, I simply said, "Thanks for everything, Candace, but I really need to come home, and I can't do it this way. Sorry."

I apologized, but I've never had any regrets. I immediately signed on with Gluskin Sheff and didn't look back. Frequently, during Q&A sessions at events in my first two years at Gluskin Sheff, I was asked, "Why on earth did you leave a multinational bank on Wall Street for a small wealth manager on Bay Street?"

"When I found out that my wife hired a pool boy," I'd say, "I knew it was time to get my ass home, especially since we don't own a swimming pool."

There's nothing wrong with a crowd-pleaser at speaking functions. I used that line until it got stale. The lesson here is to always work on new material and know when to retire the old.

More importantly, try to do the right thing when you get to that proverbial fork in the road, and never let money cloud your judgment. Nobody on earth has your back like your family does. I am thankful for the career that I have had, but I am even more grateful that it wasn't too late for me to change paths, come back home, be present with my family, and achieve more balance in my life.

CHAPTER 24

Was I Fired on the First Day?

My first day at Gluskin Sheff was not at the firm's swanky offices in downtown Toronto. Instead, I went to Langdon Hall, the renowned five-star resort, about ninety minutes southwest of the city. I have given many speeches there over the years. Gluskin Sheff was co-sponsoring a high-net-worth event at the resort, and I was scheduled to be the breakfast speaker on the Monday. Having just completed my last presentation at Merrill on the Friday prior, all I needed to do was update the logo on my slides. My views hadn't changed in the intervening days. In my introduction, I thanked the audience for attending, the organizers for setting up the event, and Ira (who was in the crowd) for giving me the weekend off.

That evening, Ira was the dinner speaker. Standing at the front of the dining hall and swirling his glass of wine, he announced, "My topic for tonight's address is this: why did Gluskin Sheff decide to hire David Rosenberg?" As all 150 people in the room turned to stare at me, I felt beads of sweat forming on my forehead. Ira did offer some compliments, but they were nuanced, backhanded, and filled with double entendres. He certainly garnered some laughs—though not from me. He concluded with this little ditty: "The question I have been fielding all day is, 'What happens if David Rosenberg starts to be wrong? What if his hot hand turns cold?' Well, my answer hasn't changed from my morning and afternoon conversations: we'll simply fire him!"

Gales of laughter erupted as I mentally retreated under the table.

A few years later, the two co-founders stepped away from their day-to-day responsibilities and handed the reins to new management teams. They still maintained offices at the company, at least they did until their lawsuit against the firm, but that's a story for another book—it didn't end well for several people. After all this, Ira stopped by my office. He mentioned that he had just done a BNN interview and, when asked a macro question, had directed the host to me instead. I responded, "Thanks very much. By the way, my hand must still be hot, or at least warm, don't you think?"

Ira asked what I meant. I reminded him of what he had said four years earlier about what would happen if my palms changed temperatures. I said, "I must be doing a good job." Ira retorted, "What makes you think that?" To which I replied, "Well, you haven't fired me yet."

"Rosenberg, you have to remember, I no longer have any executive power here. The thing is, I can't fire you!"

Nothing like a shot of confidence, right? The lesson here is that in my profession, like most others, you need a thick skin to survive.

CHAPTER 25

When You Don't Have a Plan B

While I was negotiating with the Gluskin Sheff folks about joining them, I learned that senior brass weren't thrilled with the idea of me continuing my daily report, but I convinced them it would be a win-win and made it clear that it was a condition of my employment. They relented. After all, we're talking about my stock-in-trade here.

Of course, the daily needed a new title. At that time, Gluskin Sheff's tag line was "Stubbornly Unconventional." That really spoke to me. So, the new title wasn't going to be something conventional like A.M. Notes or Morning Market Memo.

I turned to my family for the answer. Back when my parents were alive, our families—my wife, kids, sister, and her family—would meet every Sunday morning at United Bakers, a legendary dairy deli in northern Toronto—their pea, bean, and barley soup was to die for. For years, we congregated at the same table, served by Helen, whom we all adored. One Sunday at United, just before my first day at Gluskin, we were discussing what to rename my daily commentary. The debate became heated, as all our family conversations did, and still do, until Michael, the youngest of our three children, blurted out, between bites of his pizza bagel, "Breakfast with Dave."

You could hear a pin drop. Then, in unison, we all exclaimed, "That's it!"

I said to Michael, "That's so simple, yet so brilliant. What made you think of that?"

"Dad, it's pretty simple. People read your stuff over breakfast, and your name is Dave."

And that is the story of how "Breakfast with Dave" came to be, over a family breakfast on a Sunday morning twelve years ago, thanks to the spontaneity of a pre-teen.

* * *

Among the several reasons that the opportunity at Gluskin Sheff appealed to me more than, say, remaining on the "sell side" at a Canadian bank, was that I believed that gaining exposure to a "buy side" firm would broaden my experience and help my career. I wasn't wrong. I learned more in my eleven years there than in my previous twenty-two years as a bank economist.

When you become chief economist at a major Wall Street bank and receive all-star ratings in the rankings, you tend to think you have it all figured out. Check the ego at the door? Forget about it!

My time at Gluskin Sheff grounded me. My approach to presenting and communicating forecasts underwent a significant transformation.

It began during my first month at the firm. At one of the weekly investment committee meetings, I presented my macro and market forecasts for the upcoming year. After I finished, Ira Gluskin asked me:

"Rosie, what is your Plan B?"

"What??"

"What if you're wrong? You've surely been wrong in the past. Tell us, if you're wrong, where are you going to be wrong?"

I don't often stutter, but I certainly did then. I didn't have an answer.

The meeting concluded with Ira's sage advice, which has resonated with me ever since: "Rosie, if you don't have a Plan B, you don't have a plan."

Yikes! I couldn't believe how arrogant I must have seemed. It was my first opportunity to impress my new colleagues on the Gluskin Sheff investment committee and I'd presented my scenario as though it was the only possible outcome.

So, I went back to the drawing board and reformatted my presentation to include my base-case scenario, along with other scenarios that I considered reasonably probable. This meant incorporating tail risk, something I've since become quite adept at—perhaps excessively so.

I presented my most likely scenario for the economy, inflation, interest rates, the stock market, and various sectors. Then I added not just a Plan B, but a Plan C, a Plan D, and a Plan E. It took some time to sink in, but I quickly realized that there is no such thing as a sure thing, and you should never put all your eggs in one basket. It's a simple yet elegant concept, and Ira's advice has stayed with me. It's all about having a base-case view but accepting that nothing in forecasting is 100 percent certain. I assigned probabilities to the base-case and to each of the other lettered scenarios.

Sometimes, I would attend a meeting with no change to my base-case, except for a different probability estimate. In other words, it's valuable for an investor to understand how an economist's conviction level is shifting, even if the base-case remains unchanged. It's also important to estimate how the probabilities are changing for all the other outcomes. I could now attend an investment committee meeting, keep my base-case projection the same, but alter the assessed odds of it happening. I could tell the group that Plan B was now Plan C, and Plan D was now Plan B, and the portfolio managers and analysts would be scribbling notes furiously—even though I hadn't changed my base-case!

What I did was influence the shape of the probability distribution of all potential outcomes. Through this process, early in my time at Gluskin Sheff, I learned how to present an economic and financial forecast that would add more value and substance to the investment decision-making process. This wasn't a lesson I learned at Merrill Lynch. Back then, I was constantly moving from boardroom to boardroom for hourly discussions with clients, and I never really grasped how a money manager thinks: it's all about the probability curve—how perceived outcomes are shifting, and what the potential reward of being right is benchmarked against the cost of being wrong across that distribution. Had I understood this during my years at Merrill, I would have communicated a far different set of forecasts to clients. Identifying the ever-changing risks to the base-case forecast is actually more useful for an investor than the base-case itself. This goes to show that you can teach an old dog new tricks, although I was only fifty when this light bulb went off.

Spending every day for eleven years with the Gluskin Sheff investment team and in regular contact with the chief investment officers was a completely different experience than leading an economics department at a major bank. Even though I spent more time on the floor than most bank economists, I was living in an ivory tower, far removed from the action. Gluskin Sheff taught me what makes an institutional investor tick and I was able to be a more effective contributor. Furthermore, sitting with the portfolio managers day in and day out, I observed that the best were the ones who showed the greatest discipline. I was told, "Never fall in love with your portfolio," and I began to think that, as an economist, I should also "never fall in love with my base-case forecast." It won't love you back! I learned always to be on the lookout for evidence that contradicts your base-case view and to do your best to be aware of your blind spots. These are critical ingredients for success, whether you're a wealth manager, analyst, strategist, or economist.

Of course, there's a gray area between being confident in your base-case and being ready to shift to Plan B—the willingness and ability to be flexible. As I watched the portfolio managers at Gluskin Sheff trim or abandon positions because their initial markers weren't met, I learned, as an economist, to set my own guidelines for when it would be appropriate to change my call. I followed the examples of the most effective portfolio managers who exhibited that discipline and didn't let emotions get in the way: if the call wasn't working out, they would get out and move on. Those were the ones who never blew up—and that's a key element of success in the investing world because it can take years to recover from a faulty position you held for too long. Macro forecasts should be treated the same way.

There's no room for arrogance or stubbornness in forecasting, and shame on me when I'm guilty of it—although it happens; we're only human, after all.

CHAPTER 26

Rules to Remember

I owe much to Bob Farrell, the legendary technical strategist at Merrill Lynch, for shaping my views and philosophy over the decades. I was following his research all the way back in the 1980s when I was just starting out. While we only intersected at Merrill for a short while, being able to rub shoulders with Bob during my time in New York has been an inspiration to me ever since. He taught me a great deal.

Early on in my career at Merrill, I began to incorporate Bob's famous Ten Market Rules to Remember into my work. The thing about these rules is that they involve discipline, and following them can often get one labeled as a perma bear because if you aren't bulled up at all times in this business, people think you must live in a cave. I find perma bulls, as a group, to be the sort of people who have something to sell you. There's a catch, an agenda, with these folks, who always seem to be throwing caution to the wind, even when market manias morph into bubbles.

Bob was a pioneer in incorporating sentiment into technical research. He understood that investor psychology is just as important as fundamentals, liquidity, and valuations in determining whether any asset class is overextended or a terrific buying opportunity. His Ten Market Rules to Remember formed the basis for my own Economic Rules to Remember. Here are both.

Bob Farrell's Ten Market Rules to Remember:

1. Markets tend to return to the mean over time.
2. Excesses in one direction will lead to an opposite excess in the other direction.
3. There are no new eras—excesses are never permanent.
4. Exponentially rapidly rising or falling markets usually go further than you think, but they do not correct by going sideways.
5. The public buys the most at the top and the least at the bottom.
6. Fear and greed are stronger than long-term resolve.
7. Markets are strongest when they are broad and weakest when they narrow to a handful of blue-chip names.
8. Bear markets have three stages—sharp down, reflexive rebound, and a drawn-out fundamental downtrend.
9. When all the experts and forecasts agree—something else is going to happen.
10. Bull markets are more fun than bear markets.

Rosie's Ten Economic Rules to Remember:

1. In order for an economic forecast to be relevant, it must be combined with a market call. (If it doesn't translate into investable outcomes, what good is it?)
2. Never be a slave to the data. (The numbers are no substitute for astute observation of the big picture.)
3. Never fear being out of consensus. (The consensus rarely gets it right and almost always errs on the side of optimism, except at the bottom.)
4. Fall in love with your partner, not your forecast. (You need to have a backbone, but you do not want to be stubborn.)
5. Every cycle shares similarities, but no two cycles are ever completely the same. (Use the historical record judiciously.)

6. Never hide behind your model. (Incorporate your instinct, intuition, experience, and judgment, which are equally important.)
7. Always seek out non-corroborating evidence. (Check your blind spots at all times.)
8. Have respect for what the markets are telling you. (Especially listen to the bond market, which usually gets the story right.)
9. Be constantly aware of your forecast horizon. (Separate the tactical calls from the secular view.)
10. Highlight the risks to your forecasts at all times. (Build scenarios—there is no such thing as a sure thing.)

I must say that what stands out most for me in Bob Farrell's list at the time of writing are Rules #2 and #4. For mine, I am focused most on #3 and #8.

CHAPTER 27

More on the Ten Commandments

As mentioned earlier, the great Bob Farrell provided us long ago with crucial guideposts for prudent investing. I don't want to put words in Mr. Farrell's mouth, but I'd like to share my own interpretation of what this living legend was trying to teach us. Here are some further thoughts on his blueprint.

Rule #1: Markets tend to return to the mean over time.

Go back and see if a market ever failed to revert to the mean. We cannot think of a single example where this has not happened. Of course, you look at the Ibbotson chart, which shows equity prices marching higher and higher over a century, and gains seem inevitable. But one also needs to take into account, at any moment in time, price/earnings ratios, price-to-sales, and price-to-book ratios, as well as dividend yields. These are the metrics that matter to the equity shareholder with respect to expected returns. Prices-to-rents ratios and property-valuation-to-GDP ratios exhibit tremendous mean-reverting properties in the housing sector, as well. Ditto for bond-to-stock return ratios, the relative strength of small-cap stocks and equal-weight indices, sector concentrations, interest rates (both real and nominal), credit spreads, and even currencies. And remember that mean reversion necessarily means correcting two extremes—bull markets and bear markets do not correct by just going to the mean; they break well through the mean.

Rule #2: Excesses in one direction will lead to an opposite excess in the other direction.

Oil prices hit $30 per barrel in 1979, $12 per barrel in 1998, and $20 per barrel in 2002. Oil spent much of the 1980s and 1990s well below the mean, especially in real terms. That was an example of an excess below the mean, and because of that excessively low price and the dearth of production growth, oil prices inevitably broke the other way, soaring well above the mean from 2003 to present. The same example is held in the housing market bubble of nearly two decades ago, where the excess 20 percent annual price appreciation from 2000 to 2006 entered the ultimate mean-reversion process for nearly a decade. Not to mention the classic mean-reversion trade we saw in the Nifty Fifty stocks in the late 1960s, silver in the early 1980s, Japan in the late 1990s, and commercial real estate in the late 1990s. And today we have a huge price bubble in wide swaths of the US equity market (it's not just AI and tech). Unprecedented rising values are typically followed by unprecedented declining values.

Rule #3: There are no new eras—excesses are never permanent.

What happens is that at the peak of a bubble, new-era thinking and permanent-shortage beliefs begin to drive market pricing. Or how about the notion of American Exceptionalism, as if that's really something new? It is not difficult for an economist who has an understanding of how markets work to be skeptical about the new era rationalizations for why excesses are deemed to be permanent. Doesn't matter if it's "the new economy," "peak oil," "finite supply of land," "no more ocean-front property," or "new era" thinking around generative AI. Of course, timing the corrections is difficult because it is practically impossible to determine when an irrational process is going to come to a halt.

Rule #4: Exponentially rapidly rising or falling markets usually go further than you think, but they do not correct by going sideways.

The asset bubble reality of the past few years, which has gone much further than anyone expected, was induced by an extremely lax credit cycle and the massive doses of fiscal stimulus that transcended the pandemic recession. As the mania morphs into a bubble, we embark on the asymptotic or blow-the-top-off-move that marks the last gasp of the bull market.

We always talk about the credit and housing market bubble in the mid-to-late 2000s, but fail to remember that oil prices also went into an orbit of their own when they touched $146 per barrel in the summer of 2008. The prevailing view back then was that the gains made sense because of endless double-digit economic growth in China—like today, more new-era thinking.

Whatever the fundamental rationalizations of these exponentially extended markets, the reality is that what drives them is leverage, and because of that, the market cannot accommodate the extraordinary expansion of buyers and remain orderly. The same holds true when the market heads south because it cannot accommodate all the sellers. Remember what happened to tech stocks in the 2000–2002 period and to the shift from excess housing demand to excess housing supply later that decade—those are classic examples of what Farrell is talking about. Parabolic moves, or exponentially rising or falling prices, do not correct by leveling off.

Today, the real bubble is in the insatiable appetite for passive-index investing, which we know won't last indefinitely since nothing does. What makes this cycle different is that most owners of equity have no clue what they actually have in their portfolio. Inevitably, to get all the people out, the asset in question has to go from unbelievably expensive to extremely cheap, as Nasdaq did from 2000 to 2002, or vice versa.

Rule #5: The public buys the most at the top, the least at the bottom.

This particular rule simply clarifies that human nature commonly expresses itself in linear thinking. It has always been difficult for the general public to sell things that are going up in price or to buy things that have done poorly despite attractive valuations. Investment assets are not the same as asparagus: as the price of asparagus goes up, people buy fewer spears or opt for spinach. In the investment world, people buy or sell investments because they are hopeful that either the trend will continue to be up, or concerned that the trend will continue to be down.

Rule #6: Fear and greed are stronger than long-term resolve.

In the late 1990s, investors were schooled in value investing and preservation of capital. They abhorred speculation, yet found themselves powerless to avoid overweighting aggressive-growth tech stocks. This was an instance in which greed became stronger than long-term resolve. We have this on our hands today to an extent that is virtually unprecedented with the dominant Magnificent Seven stocks (Apple, Microsoft, Alphabet, Amazon, Meta, Nvidia, and Tesla).

It goes without saying that in the recent past, many investors lamented that they had dramatically reduced their equity holdings by 2002, only to see the S&P 500 more than double in the ensuing five years. The experience of that roller coaster from peak to trough and back makes it especially difficult to pay attention to fundamentals when the market experiences such intense volatility. This is what lies in our future because the move from peak greed (where we are now) to peak fear comes next. The nature of markets has not changed because of AI. It is the nature of the markets (as opposed to company business models) that they are driven by emotion. You would know what I mean by emotion if I were to print all the client comments that landed in my inbox over this past year.

This rule is vital for understanding how sentiment drives asset pricing. The herd mentality. The problem is that it would be very unusual for any bull or bear market to end prior to the public abandoning its long-term resolve, whether out of greed for continued asset inflation, or fear for further price declines. Watch what happens when the S&P 500 finally does hit its peak. At that time, the effort to ignore the fundamentals and remain fully invested, at least according to Bob Farrell's Market Rules to Remember, is unlikely to be successful. Resistance is futile.

One of the things that we need to be looking for before we turn bullish at the future market trough, based on our view of how the market works, is evidence that the abandonment of long-term resolve is in favor of fear. Once it is apparent that fear has overwhelmed long-term resolve to remain invested, it will be appropriate to turn bullish, but not before. In addition, duly note that the early stages of bull markets are typically characterized by lingering fear even in the face of improving asset prices and fundamentals. Best to pack this away for the onset of the next bear market, which, again, is inevitable, even though nobody seems to believe it will happen (the same goes for the economy—recessions somehow are a relic of the past).

Rule #7: Markets are strongest when they are broad, and weakest when they narrow to a handful of blue-chip names.

This was most certainly true in that 2006–2008 period in the commodity bubble, when oil was the only raw material price hitting new highs. Before that, the acceleration in home prices was limited to just a few cities at the bubble peak (i.e., Charlotte, Seattle, Boston, and New York). In terms of equities, go back to the 2000 peak in the tech stock bubble, and one can see that the performance was almost entirely driven by the price action in Intel, Microsoft, Sun, and Cisco. That was an indication that the market was weak. From a technical standpoint, breadth was narrow. We actually have a similar condition on our hands today, where the ratio of the equal-weight S&P 500 to the cap-weight index is back to where it was in November 2008.

Conversely, when the market price/earnings ratio bottomed at eight times back in the late 1970s and early 1980s, growth stocks like Merck and Pfizer were selling at twelve or fourteen multiples and cyclicals such as Ford and G.E. were selling at three-to-five-times earnings. In other words, the whole market was cheap and nobody wanted to own it (back to Rule #5). When the secular bull market began in 1982, practically all stocks were experiencing multiple expansion.

At the recent market peak in 2007, we were once again down to a relatively narrow list of individual stocks and industry groups leading the market. This was the era of the "decoupling theme" of globally exposed stocks (back to Rule #3), in which the rest of the world was going to buoy multinational companies even if the US went into recession. A snapshot of 2007 in many equity markets suggests that the narrowing of leadership is not altogether unlike what we experienced back in 2000. And, dare I say, we have something eerily similar on our hands today.

Rule #8: Bear markets have three stages: sharp down, reflexive rebound, and a drawn-out fundamental downtrend.

This rule is important in terms of its application to the equity market performance around the Global Financial Crisis. We witnessed a sharp decline in equity prices from 2000 to 2002, followed by a reflexive rebound. Although the up-move did return the broad market to new highs, it was reminiscent of the sharp bounce between 1932 and 1936 (although that up-move was even more pronounced). So, we could argue that we had a sharp down (2000–2002), a reflexive rebound (2002–2007), and then a classic long and drawn-out decline to a fresh low by early 2009. In any case, always remember that secular trends, whether bullish or bearish, never go in a straight line indefinitely.

Rule #9: When all experts and forecasts agree, something else is going to happen.

On the surface, this rule sounds somewhat cynical. It is not. Simply put, tops are made at that point of maximum bullishness; bottoms are made at the point of maximum bearishness (as Sir John Templeton once put it). The more universal the bullishness or bearishness, the more likely it is that we are at an extreme. It always has to be a bit of a concern when everyone agrees that the outlook is rosy; and you have to be salivating at the prospects that all the bad news is more than fully priced in when everybody is depressed and pessimistic (i.e., "The Death of Equities" front cover of the August 1979 *BusinessWeek*). Such is the miserable life of the contrarian: always the skunk at the picnic when the market is going sky-high, and the person nobody listens to when the markets are bottoming and fundamentals and valuations become attractive.

Rule #10: Bull markets are more fun than bear markets.

This rule is obvious and was thrown in for fun. No doubt everyone feels giddy in bull markets. Paper wealth is created and consumers tend to spend more based on the rise in household net worth. Bear markets destroy wealth and in the process undermine confidence. No fun.

That said, there are ways to mitigate the misery of a bear market. One is to price the risk in the marketplace and have a keen eye on capital preservation—that's something that should never go out of style, especially when times are good. The lesson for market economists is to try and dull the pain during bear market episodes and control the infectious exuberance that accompanies bull market phases. Our role is to provide a realistic assessment of the current macro situation and the outlook in order to provide some basis on which to make asset allocation decisions. At this stage, our work is still advocating a conservative equity and overweight fixed-income strategy. We are diligently looking for signs that will turn us bullish on stocks, but with current stock market valuations reflecting an expectation of 20 percent annual average increases in earnings-per-share growth for the next five years, the bar is high.

With all that in mind, I continue to follow closely and adhere to the guideposts expressed in Bob Farrell's Ten Market Rules to Remember.

CHAPTER 28

Drinking Through the Pandemic

Like most people, I've been asked how I endured the pandemic. My answer is always the same: wine.

Good wine. And lots of it. Not to the point where it clouds my judgment, despite what some may think after reading my forecasts.

I wasn't always a wine guy. I used to prefer beer and scotch. I developed a taste for the grape when I started working at BMO-Nesbitt in 1994. Sherry Cooper's spouse, Peter, co-owned a vineyard in South Africa. She got me hooked at our very first departmental dinner. Before that, I couldn't distinguish between a Barolo and a Beaujolais.

My love for wine truly blossomed when I moved to New York City to work for Merrill Lynch. This was in 2002, just as the housing and mortgage boom gained momentum. Every firm on Wall Street was making enormous profits and marketing budgets were exploding. While I returned home to Toronto on the weekends, the various sales teams took me out with clients virtually every night from Monday to Thursday. It's a miracle I didn't weigh 300 pounds at that time. Dinners were accompanied by exceptional wines—the best of the best. Although the discussions primarily centered on the macroeconomy and the markets, they invariably included commentary on the wines being served. The sales force and their clients were quite knowledgeable. While I dominated the conversation when it came to GDP, the ISM index, and the S&P 500, I kept quiet (yes, I can do that), listening and observing as the conversation shifted to wine.

I recall during my first few months in NYC, the hedge fund sales team took me and their top ten clients to the basement cellar of a well-known Italian restaurant in Greenwich Village. They hired a sommelier and a cheese expert. I was instructed to avoid acronyms, keep my remarks brief, and be light, erudite, and funny (I can do that, too). I believe I kept my remarks to around ten minutes (a first for everything). Afterward, the sommelier described the wines being served, from Brunello to Barolo to the big Tuscans. The cheese expert gave us a lesson I'll never forget. I can still taste the gorgonzola, parmigiano, and mascarpone. I remember standing there, after finishing my spiel, swirling my Brunello, and thinking, "Wow, and they pay me for this, too."

I owe a debt of gratitude to Paul Vancura, a senior figure on the institutional sales desk and a good friend, for elevating my wine knowledge. Paul no longer drinks and has become extremely health-conscious (he's even a kickboxer), but in those days, after a heavy day of marketing, we would go to this amazing wine bar on Hudson Street in Tribeca, with him as the teacher and me as the student.

I never acquired a taste for pinot noir until one evening when Paul told me my problem was buying too much plonk, and that for this fickle wine, you really do have to trade up. Tastings of Flowers and Etude were all it took. When I came back in 2009, these two wines became legendary at Gluskin Sheff. I have Paul to thank for it.

Starting in 2011, I began taking spring trips to Napa with various friends. I highly recommend that anyone planning a Napa trip contact Ona and Dan Marks, who run Designated Drivers

Napa. They will take excellent care of you and get you into small, boutique vineyards—tomorrow's Screaming Eagle, but at a fraction of the price. I really like Old World wines, but I simply adore Napa wines—the big, bold ones, from Howell Mountain Cabernet to Russian River Pinot. Bring them on.

In some sense, I can say that wine actually gave me the courage to finally start my own business. Back in the spring of 2017, Leslie Rudd, a highly successful entrepreneur, philanthropist, and proprietor of one of the most amazing wineries in the valley—the Rudd Family Samantha's Oakville cab is sensational—invited me to his office for lunch on his incredible property. I confided in Leslie about my yearning to start my own research consulting firm, but admitted that the fear of failure was standing in my way. As he poured me another glass of his legendary cabernet, he pointed to a framed picture on his wall, bearing these words: "If you weren't afraid, what would you be doing?"

I have never forgotten that moment. Even after a full bottle of his signature cab, I got the message right away. Fear not. Carpe diem. Live bravely and boldly.

Leslie passed away in May 2018, but his legacy and his wines live on, as does my passion for the grape, which, late in life, helped me confront and conquer my fear of hanging my shingle at Rosenberg Research.

CHAPTER 29

Dancing on the Head of a Pin

The one thing that drew me to economics as a profession was that it involved coursework that covered the entire gamut of math, psychology, and history. History was always my strongest suit. To this day.

And the one thing we know about history is that capitalism and democracy are always dancing on the head of a pin. Their combination is what made the American experiment so successful. But it only works when there is social stability and the low end of the income spectrum is not left behind. The prolonged economic imbalance we've been experiencing for decades now, with real labor compensation running at a fraction of real unit profits growth, is both unhealthy and unsustainable.

The historical record going back thousands of years shows that the collapse of empires is associated with unsustainable debts, inflation, income disparities, and wealth gaps. I find it a sad state of affairs that what dominates the headlines and everyone's attention today is the reshaping of the global trading network, the White House's battles with elite universities, and the immigration file. Meanwhile, there is not a peep from the government, or indeed from almost anyone else, on the one critical issue that jeopardizes our social stability, now and in the future:

> Higher inequality increases the stock of savings and demand for riskier assets, which can explain why inequality is positively related

> to nonbank sector size and debt as well as higher valuations of riskier assets relative to GDP. In addition, higher savings of the rich have also been shown to increase dissaving of both the rest of the households and the government through a higher supply of credit, linking this same mechanism to overborrowing of lower-income households
>
> While we do not attempt to make causal claims, we argue that inequality may exacerbate vulnerabilities that have been shown to propagate shocks in the financial system and worsen real outcomes.

Those quotes are from "Inequality and financial sector vulnerabilities," a report published on April 19, 2024, by two Federal Reserve researchers, Anni T. Isojaervi and Sam Jerow. To put it in layman's terms, wealth is concentrating at the top, excess savings are flowing into markets, inflating asset prices. Credit is abundant and often cheap, encouraging more borrowing across the economy and leaving the whole system more fragile for when conditions inevitably turn.

Forewarned is forearmed, as my maternal grandmother used to tell me. This issue, the massive gap in income and wealth, has gone unaddressed by policymakers year in and year out, irrespective of whether Democrats or Republicans are in power. It is not the foreign producer and exporter who have stolen jobs from America and hollowed out the middle class. It is the entire tax system, especially concerning where government subsidies and support are directed. The simple fact is that the government never made adequate efforts to retool and retrain the workers who were most affected by globalization. It is not globalization that is at fault. It is years of neglect at the highest levels of the public sector.

I have studied the data depicting the record or near-record shares of income and wealth possessed by the top 1 percent—I happen to be among them, but somehow I don't feel too comfortable about that. I would recommend against saying "let them eat cake." All of us in the top 1 percent, or top 0.1 percent, should recognize and be sensitive to the incontrovertible fact that capitalism needs social stability and democracy to survive. But we are on a slippery slope and have been for some time. The marriage of democracy and capitalism requires constant nurturing, not neglect. And, again, the historical record shows that the collapse of empires is associated with unsustainable debts, inflation, and income disparities, as well as extreme wealth gaps, all of which we have.

We need to constantly remind ourselves that capitalism needs democracy, and democracy needs social stability. Nothing I see policy-wise right now tells me we are heading in a very good direction. This is the problem with the 2025 tariff war and the Big Beautiful Budget Bill. They offer nothing to the "little guy." If anything, they only make matters worse. The fact that the president and his vice president focus so much on crypto and so little on diverging income and wealth levels is worrying. And since nobody wants to talk about this issue, especially in our financial industry, I will pick up the mantle. I am a free-market capitalist and want to ensure its longevity for my children.

We need to face the issues. There is a huge imbalance in the economy and it is only getting worse with time. The labor share of income has hit the lowest level on record. When you get to two standard-deviation events in critical ratios like the labor share of income or, at the other end of the spectrum, profit margins and income concentration at the highest echelons, you know we have hit unstable extremes. I hate to say it, but there is a reason why Bernie Sanders is far and away the most popular political figure in Washington with a 69 percent approval rating, and real strength among youth.

From 1950 to 1980, productivity growth averaged just over 2 percent annually, and real worker compensation per hour matched that pace. Something happened in 1980. I have often said that Ronald Reagan was the greatest president of our time, but while the Gipper had exceptional leadership and communication skills, I'm not so sure anymore. Because it was his policies that got the ball rolling here, especially on tax reform. Top marginal corporate tax rates were 46 percent then and are 21 percent today. Everyone embraced the reforms at the time, notably on Wall Street. Remember what Gordon Gekko told us about greed being good? Yet since then productivity has averaged 2 percent annually, while real work-based incomes have averaged less than half that pace at 1 percent annually. Compound that divergence over a forty-five-year period and it amounts to a whole lot of money.

You see how dangerous this is, right? In a balanced economy, workers should be reaping the fruits of their labor. Their real compensation growth should match the labor component of productivity growth that they bring to their employers. From 1980 to 2025, this did not happen. Workers were doing their jobs: their productivity growth remained constant at 2 percent annually, but their compensation lagged at 1 percent. Doesn't that bother anyone? Access to the services sector in Asia, or being able to sell more beef in the UK are more important than this? Really? Does no one give a damn? I suggest we don't.

In any event, the gap is not sustainable. Putting the blame on foreign trading partners is gaslighting to an extreme. It amazes me what short shrift this topic receives.

Who benefited from the continued expansion in labor productivity if it wasn't the workers? It was the owners. From 1950 to 1980, unit profits in the nonfinancial corporate sector rose at a 2 percent average annual rate. Businesses and workers shared equally in the productivity gains. But since 1980, unit profits growth doubled to nearly a 4 percent average annual rate.

I mentioned earlier that since 1980, the top marginal corporate tax rate has plunged from 46 percent to 21 percent. In the personal tax sector, the rate is down from 70 percent to 37 percent. The share of revenues coming from the personal sector has stayed roughly at 50 percent, but the corporate share has gone from 14 percent to 10 percent. There definitely is something wrong here. It seems to me that within the personal sector, the tax system is simply not progressive enough.

The tax system needs to be addressed. As it has been constructed, it cannot support the grotesque levels of public sector expenditures. The US government has not balanced its books in a quarter century and since that time, the level of debt has ballooned by $30 trillion. Federal debt has soared fivefold.

There is your answer to the question about the veracity of the Laffer Curve and whether tax cuts end up paying for themselves, as politicians and some economists falsely claim to be the case. As a share of GDP, the debt has mushroomed from 55 percent when Bill Clinton left office in 2000 to 130 percent today. In that timeframe, the tax revenue share of GDP has gone from 20 percent to below 17 percent. That has to change. And it is foolhardy to believe we can grow out of this, even with the AI craze.

Nothing adds up. The price/earnings multiple is twenty-three times, meaning stocks are expensive. The VIX (or volatility index) is below 20, meaning markets are calm. The yield spread between junk bonds and US Treasuries is less than 300 basis points, meaning investors think risk is low. How can there be this much complacency in so unstable an environment? In a word: denial. The explosion in debt has occurred as income inequality is reaching unprecedented levels. That means instability layered on instability. The case for gold is front and center, and it has little to do with tariff uncertainty.

There was a very clever way to keep the low end of the income spectrum feeling it could afford the American Dream even after real wages in 1980 began lagging their productivity contribution by half, and the labor share of national income dwindled to record lows. By deregulating the financial sector and allowing banks and other lenders to plug Main Street with debt. The outstanding level of debt in the household sector has surged by a factor of ten since 1980 to $20 trillion. The number of households has only expanded 70 percent over that period. In 1970, personal debt, including loans and mortgages, was $7,000 per household. In 1980, it went up to $17,000. A decade later, after a proliferation of financial innovation and ever-increasing access to credit, that number rose by 1990 to $38,000. Then to $70,000 in 2000, $125,000 in 2010 (after a debt-laden mortgage boom), and $125,000 in 2020. It now sits at $150,000. Insane. You need to have your head examined if you're going long on a consumer finance company.

In 1970, credit cards were a $3-billion business. Only high-income earners with a credit score could access a card and they had one American Express card. It was a status symbol. Even in 1980, it was just a $50-billion business. Today? Try $1.3 trillion! Did you know that the outstanding number of credit cards in the US now tops 630 million? The population of those sixteen and older is 163 million! So, hubby has a card. Wife has a card. The teenage kid has a card. And Fido has a card. Each household has four different credit cards. This, along with government-insured mortgages, encouraged the personal debt sector, particularly people in the low- and middle-income classes, to replace the incomes they should have received from their productivity—money that was instead diverted to profits—with easy access to credit.

How can this possibly end well? I'm not sure there is anything safe to invest in today, outside of gold (maybe I should include Bitcoin too, but I don't own any of it). Now that the Fed has raised rates by 400 basis points from the cycle lows and is leaving monetary policy deliberately tight, we are seeing the strains beginning to surface. Delinquency rates have surged on credit cards and auto loans. It has spread to student debt and even mortgage late-payment rates are edging higher. Consumer confidence for the lowest income cohort has plummeted to all-time lows.

Because young adults are saddled with so much debt, and have few job or income prospects, their confidence levels have also plumbed the depths. They confront an additional problem, which is that the dream of owning a home is just that—a dream. Government policy has promoted so much asset inflation in the form of excessive home prices—it isn't just the stock market—that homeowner affordability today is more stretched than at any other time in the past forty years. A median starter home price now averages out to $342,000. Median incomes for this group stand at $68,000. Qualifying income for a mortgage loan is $100,000. How on earth can young people ever move out of their parents' basement? There are over 24 million Americans between the ages of eighteen and thirty-four still living at home. Nearly one in three!

As a result, they are getting married later and having fewer kids, which is radically reshaping the country's population profile. The population strains will only be exacerbated by tighter immigration rules. Household formation for twenty-somethings is in a fundamental bear market, and average family size has fallen to record depressed levels as birth rates and fertility rates have declined to record lows. This is a different issue than income inequality, to be sure, but the debt-fueled surge in home prices that is keeping young people from striking out on their own is another critical imbalance that I sense is going to upset the apple cart when it comes to social stability.

It's time to stop this obsession with blaming foreign trading partners for our problems at home and start focusing on the real problems. They are homegrown. The tax system has not only failed to cover the insane levels of government spending, which have somehow been allowed to surge more than 50 percent above the level immediately preceding the pandemic in 2019, but has also failed to prevent income inequalities from rising further to unprecedented levels. Means-testing social security or widening the bands of the income tax rate schedules have somehow become taboo, as has the idea of tightening the bands between net effective corporate rates and those in the personal sector. And that, my friends, will carry with it the laws of unintended consequences. Not now, perhaps, but in the future.

To put an investment spin on this, we have on our hands global trade uncertainty (and the tariffs, again, disproportionately hurt low-income households), fiscal instability, obvious geopolitical instability, and the social instability that is growing out of everything I outlined earlier. And the allure of physical gold is perfectly correlated with instability.

CHAPTER 30

Not So Tiny Bubbles

At the time of writing, it is clear to me that we are in a classic equity bubble, and as Bob Farrell posited, these episodes typically go further than you think. It's typical of human nature. When greed becomes the primary emotion, which is clearly the case today, everybody wants to stay invested and thinks they are nimble enough to time the market's peak.

There is no doubt that we have experienced a major shift in the innovation curve with the AI boom, but over the centuries, investors have generally over-extrapolated what future growth, productivity, and returns on capital will be down the road. We have reached a point where valuations are so extreme that they are pricing in a 15 percent average annual growth in earnings per share for the next five years, double the historical norm. It's not impossible, but it's improbable, and at this point, the risk is one of disappointment given what is already baked into equity prices.

We can check the boxes for all seven bubble characteristics: valuations, leverage, market positioning, expectations, sentiment, concentration, and over-ownership. I don't know why anyone should be surprised. From the steam engine to the cotton gin to the railway to electricity to the transistor to the mainframe computer to the Internet, investment euphoria and asset price bubbles always follow a major shift in the technology curve. With the generative AI boom, things are playing out as they always have, with investors overestimating, in their Gordon Gekko lust for greed, what the size of the available market will ultimately be.

I wouldn't bother trying to time the peak. Just know that there will be a bubble peak, there always is, and the aftermath is horrible. Another investing legend, Jeremy Grantham, said on one of my recent webcasts that a bubble is defined by a two-standard-deviation event. Well, I can safely conclude that the mean, median, and mode are pressing against a two-standard-deviation event versus their historical norms. And anyone who knows me and my investing style knows that I will never participate in, let alone chase, a two-sigma event. This is when you know that the bull market is in extra innings.

Over 70 percent of the US household asset mix is now concentrated in the equity market (only 8 percent is in bonds, but who wants a margin of safety in their portfolio, correct?). That tops the peak numbers that presaged the last three recessionary bear markets of 2001, 2008, and 2020. On their own, peak numbers don't produce recessions, but such radically high exposure causes the bear market to be severe as everyone moves defensively to rebalance their portfolios into the relative safety of cash and bonds.

Vanguard's data are rather shocking in this regard: workers in their late thirties had 88 percent of their 401(k)s concentrated in stocks last year. Meanwhile—get this—401(k) investors in their early sixties had boosted their allocations to stocks of an unheard-of 60 percent. This is about double the exposure these folks should have in their portfolio. In target-date funds, which move money from stocks to bonds as retirement approaches, the average equity allocation for workers just beginning their careers was 92 percent at the end of 2024. This speaks to an equity culture in which everybody is loaded up on risk all at the same time. Talk about throwing caution to the wind.

The fact that this aggressiveness is working today is a poor excuse not to diversify or rebalance. Yet in today's investing environment, that advice is met with a yawn and a shrug of the shoulders. The idea of managing risk has been thrown into the wastepaper basket. While not a problem today, I can guarantee it will become a big problem down the road as everyone attempts to time an exit at the peak.

The Shiller CAPE multiple has expanded by almost 5 points since May 2025 to 39.5 times earnings, which exceeds every prior bubble peak in the past century outside of the unprecedented tech mania in the late 1990s and early 2000s. This compares to the 1929 bubble peak of 33 times earnings, the Nifty Fifty peak in the late 1960s of 24 times, and the 1987 pre-crash peak of 18 times. The average bubble peak in this valuation metric is 26 times. We are now pressing against 40 times. We are in the stratosphere. Historically, when we have seen the CAPE behave this way, the bubble lasted a median of sixteen months (as per Bob Farrell, "going further than you think"). The CAPE first emerged as a two-standard-deviation event in June 2024 when it was just a tick below 35 times (it is now approaching a three-standard-deviation event). The clock is ticking.

The surge in valuations has coincided with indices of investor sentiment soaring off the charts. That happens to be a contrary negative. An overwhelming consensus. Herd mentality. The madness of crowds. A red flag. When you are priced for perfection, and are expecting perfection, disappointment always follows because the world is not perfect. The major point here is how extreme things have become.

But is anyone listening?

This extreme level of complacency/exuberance is underscored in the credit markets as well, where investment-grade spreads have recently tightened to the lowest levels since 1998. History shows that neither this level of spreads, nor the CAPE multiple of nearly 40 times, is ever sustained, although they can certainly last several months before everyone tries to exit at the same time. Not a worry for anyone today, since most people believe they are effective market timers. Or maybe they believe they can outlast corrections, or that bear markets in risk assets are relics of the past.

The bottom line is that a price bubble is by definition a market that loses touch with underlying fundamentals, where all the metrics—price-to-earnings ratios, price-to-sales ratios, price-to-book ratios, the Shiller CAPE, the Buffett Indicator—trade north of two standard deviations. Not that the earnings fundamentals are not good, but that the price action is double the underlying earnings streams. Whatever it is that comes out of the AI boom in terms of the future impact on productivity, the economy, and earnings, the reality, after you do the math in backing out the message from Mr. Market, is that the expectation embedded in today's valuations is highly unlikely. It is not impossible, but it still represents a one-in-ten event. The last time we saw things lined up this way was back in the late 1990s tech boom. The Internet, as we all know, was a game-changer from a personal and commercial standpoint, but remember what happened to super-inflated expectations from 2000 to 2003 as they reverted to the mean after hitting an extreme.

CHAPTER 31
Yes, I Can Do Bullish

I was invited to a Waratah Capital Advisors event in the autumn of 2025. I was part of a panel, along with Waratah co-founder and former Gluskin Sheff colleague Brad Dunkley, and the topic was gold (silver, too) and Canadian mining stocks. It was a terrific event and the ballroom was filled. But unlike today's AI conferences, whipped-up affairs reminiscent of the late 1990s Internet frenzy, there was no shortage of skepticism at this one. Which is healthy and tells me that the gold market is far from a bubble. At a manic peak, enthusiasm knows no bounds, and everyone is all in.

The folks at Waratah are rapidly building a huge position in the miners. We are aligned on the view that they have a bright future, and what makes me even more emboldened is that Brad and his team are the crème de la crème of portfolio managers in Canada—among the most unique, out-of-the-box investors I have met in my forty years in the business.

Brad left Gluskin Sheff in 2010, and this year he is celebrating the fifteenth anniversary at the firm he created. Over time, some of the best talent at Gluskin Sheff left to join Brad in building Waratah. It has turned into an enormous success. I told Brad at the event that I forgave him a long time ago for not putting an offer in front of me.

I also told the crowd what happened back in 2010 when I was at Gluskin Sheff, not long after Brad left for greener pastures. I was asked by somebody very senior at the firm: "Dave, you're so bearish! Can't you write about something you like?"

I said, "Sure."

And I did. I wrote an opus on the outlook for gold and the mining group. The senior guy came back to my office after proofing it—everything I did at Gluskin Sheff was double or triple proofed before going out, which is why establishing my own firm has been such an empowering experience. He said, "You can't publish this!"

"Why not?"

"Because we don't own any gold stocks."

I muttered under my breath: "Well, why don't we?"

The price of gold was around $1,000 per ounce at the time of that report, which went nowhere. The day I started Rosenberg Research in early 2020, gold had been a core strategy of ours. The gold price has more than doubled since then. What makes all this even more interesting, humorous in fact, is that the gold price has more than tripled since I penned that report back in 2010. I should have kept it for old time's sake. Maybe there is a chance that Gluskin Sheff (rest in peace) would still be around today had it actually done what Waratah is doing right now—aggressively building a position in an asset class that is in a bona fide secular bull market.

It's not too late. More like the third inning. The real play is in gold mining stocks (silver, too), as they do not need the current bullion price of nearly $3,700 per ounce, or even our peak forecast of $6,000 per ounce, to make money in this equity sector because it is discounting a price level of $2,700 per ounce.

Unlike investors in the AI space, the folks involved in the gold trade have no expectation that the current gold price will be maintained. They are de facto pricing in an underlying commodity level that is more than 25 percent below where it is today. The overriding message is that the gold equity sector is undervalued even after the recent run around a 40 percent price/earnings discount to the overall market and a 0.6 times price/

earnings-to-growth ratio versus around two times for both the S&P 500 and TSX. It remains an under-owned asset class.

We get criticized all the time for not having been bulled up on the S&P 500 or the high-flying tech sector. Guilty. Instead, we have been long the gold sector and are happy to report that the TSX subindex has risen by nearly 90 percent over the past year and added some serious alpha to the market performance. What has the S&P 500 done in the past year? Try up 17 percent, and the S&P 500 tech sector is up 28 percent. Gold/silver and mining stocks make up well over 20 percent of the Rosie Macro Fund. We have published several reports on the outlook for gold and gold miners over these past few years. It feels good to only have the research proofed for facts or typos, as opposed to being worried about whether or not we own the sector.

CHAPTER 32

Money Where Mouth Is

I've carried the perma bear label for many years, mostly because a whole lot of people conflate risk management, diversification, and capital preservation with bearishness, whereas I see these things as nothing more than prudent wealth building. But let's assume the masses are right and that yours truly is a perma bear. The question is, does said perma bear make you money? The answer is yes, and there is proof. It's not like I advocate for a portfolio of canned tuna, baked beans, barbed wire, and a sawed-off shotgun.

I'm constantly asked how I would grade my track record over the decades. It's not really a fair question since not every forecast was born equally—there are big calls and little calls. My usual reply is that if I ever make it to Cooperstown for economics, it will be for my home runs as opposed to at-bats. But three years ago, I had a eureka moment. Why not start a model portfolio, seeded with my own money, and put my money where my mouth is? Then we can see in real time how perma bear David Rosenberg performs when he invests around his macro and market views.

This whole process of holding my feet to the fire has actually helped make me an even more disciplined economist and strategist. It requires I be disciplined at all times, never stubborn, never hanging onto a bad call longer than necessary, always being ready to take chips off the table, and that I repel greed at all costs. I can't fall in love with my forecasts or my portfolios because they will not always love me back.

With that in mind, the decisions on what goes into the Rosie Macro Fund come down to my own personal views, the recommendations from our monthly Strategizer model, and the firm's secular investment thematics. To keep costs low and liquidity high, the holdings are all in various ETFs. I would hazard to say that half the model is "buy and hold" insofar as it reflects our longer-term views, and half is tactical to take advantage of any mispricing worth exploiting in the capital markets.

As an aside, at the time of this writing, the model portfolio has generated a net positive return since the early 2023 inception of around 60 percent. That roughly matched the S&P 500 with 40 percent of the volatility, and without having owned one Magnificent Seven stock!

So much for being a perma bear.

CHAPTER 33

Crediting My Role Models

My first three years after university, spent at the Canada Mortgage and Housing Corporation (CMHC) in Ottawa, haven't warranted much discussion in this book. CMHC, a government agency, quickly revealed to me that government work wasn't my calling. The people were pleasant, and I had an excellent boss, Denis Myette, one of the few truly great ones in my career. However, the workplace lacked energy. Despite rapid promotions and the perception by upper management that I had a promising future there, the environment was far too bureaucratic and slow for my taste. Denis and I spent years developing a report recommending that the government withdraw from selling mortgage insurance, given the thriving private sector alternatives at the time. We hoped our report would reach the federal cabinet for consideration. Instead, it gathered dust on some mid-level assistant deputy minister's desk. I still remember Denis punching the wall next to a stairwell when we received the news. I was amazed his fist didn't go right through the drywall. He punched the wall, and I punched out, heading to Bay Street.

The Bank of Nova Scotia is where I really cut my teeth as a street economist, and being part of the Big Bang global financial sector reforms in the second half of the 1980s was incredibly exciting. I learned a great deal from Warren Jestin and Aron Gampel about connecting "macro" to the "markets." That message, to always attach a market call to a macro forecast, has served me well to this day.

Some of you may also wonder why my six years at BMO Nesbitt Burns, from early 1994 to late 1999, receive little attention here. I must admit that working for Sherry Cooper was taxing, especially given the high turnover in her department and the constant uncertainty about one's job security. Even Robert Spector came close once for not delivering the euro slideshow she expected. I was once placed on probation for being quoted in *Barron's*, an achievement she had coveted. There are many stories to tell, but they are best kept private. Ultimately, Sherry and I had a functional professional relationship. While she didn't teach me anything about economics, she did teach me how to add spice to a presentation. Her slide shows in the 1990s were legendary. She delivered a very slick presentation. Warren and Aron provided the substance, and Sherry the flair. This benefited me, helping me make my presentations both informative and engaging. Moreover, as the only female chief economist on Bay Street, and with the added street cred of having worked for Paul Volcker at the Federal Reserve in the early 1980s, she was highly sought after. Even the crumbs that fell from her plate were a full meal for me. Despite her insecurities, at least with me, and her unfounded belief that I was after her job, Sherry gave me a great deal of latitude and exposure, without which I never would have been noticed by Merrill Lynch Canada. I am eternally grateful for that.

* * *

This brings me to Don Coxe. I met Don in early 1994 when I joined BMO Nesbitt Burns. He had been a household name in capital markets for years. I admire him as much as I did Bob Farrell. Don began his career in 1972 and, by the time we met, had already held numerous executive positions in portfolio management and financial research. At the time, he was chairman and chief strategist of Harris Investment Management, based in Chicago and part of the BMO group of companies. Don was renowned for his brilliant, insightful presentations, which always drew a packed house, and for his monthly publication, Basic Points, a Bay Street staple.

Don was arguably the most creative thinker I have ever known, possessing an uncanny ability to distill complex issues into elegant investment ideas. His writing was also exceptional. Don and Sherry used to do an annual show for BMO Nesbitt fixed-income clients at the Royal Ontario Museum. The legendary chef, Jamie Kennedy, provided the food and lived up to his stellar reputation, and the bar overflowed with top-shelf wine and liquor. (It was at the bar at one of these events that I met future CEO Bill Downe, who told me to start publishing my own daily newsletter, a critical turning point in my career.) Sherry would present one of her classic slide shows, while Don, without notes, would weave history, philosophy (including Shakespeare, whom he could quote in his sleep, and the occasional Greek tragedy), and politics into his market thesis. He always concluded with actionable ideas.

Studying Don, I gained a new tutor in how to be naturally interesting and informative. He was the best speaker of all time, or at least the best I have ever seen. Don and I became fast friends. Because of the age difference, I thought of him as an uncle. He was remarkably generous with his time, and I learned a great deal. While Ira Gluskin and Gerry Sheff both taught me about effective communication, Don helped me most with the delivery. In my later years at BMO Nesbitt, Don and I traveled together numerous times and tag-teamed on the podium, mostly in the Midwest. I had a canned presentation, but I once saw him give a breakfast, lunch, and dinner talk to three different sets of clients, each presentation completely unique, even though they closed with the same conclusion. He was the only colleague I was ever associated with who completely wowed me with his presentation style and writing skills, although Warren Jestin was not far behind him.

I recall my last trip with Don to Indianapolis in 1999. After the dinner presentation, we took a long walk downtown—standard fare—with Don lighting up a cigar as we decompressed. During that last walk, I confided in Don that I had received an offer from Merrill Lynch Canada to become their chief economist and strategist. I recall a sense of sadness from him, and while he tried to encourage me to reconsider, he knew my mind was already made up. We kept in touch frequently over the years. Like me, he started his own business (Coxe Advisors). A few years ago, he was a guest on one of my webcasts. We still talk every now and then, and his influence on my thinking about markets and talking about markets has stayed with me to this day.

* * *

Last November, while vacationing abroad, I received an email from Doug Porter, chief economist of the Bank of Montreal, a friend and former Bay Street colleague, informing me of Bob Brooks' sudden passing. I was totally discombobulated and since then, Bob has popped into my head every day.

Throughout the 1980s and 1990s, Bob Brooks was a senior executive at the Bank of Nova Scotia and a Bay Street titan. Everyone in the financial markets knew Bob and he commanded respect from all. On a personal level, he significantly impacted my career path at a young age.

It was in October 1987, when I began at the Bank of Nova Scotia, that I first met Bob. I split the morning meetings with my boss, Aron Gampel, and we would walk across the expansive trading floor, speaking with the markets people in foreign exchange, money market, fixed-income, precious metals, and equities. These discussions usually began at 7:30 a.m., followed by the 8:15 a.m. meeting when all the department heads convened in a conference room. Bob Brooks always chaired that meeting, and when he entered, usually last, the banter ceased and the business began. Each department head succinctly summarized the overnight market activity and anticipated the day's likely events. Finally, the economist, either Aron or I, would provide our macro view and data interpretation.

Frankly, having just spent the prior three years as a housing economist at the CMHC in Ottawa, I was out of my depth at the 8:15 a.m. meetings. I knew next to nothing about the financial markets—housing start data, maybe, but the market for overnight swaps, not so much. It took me many months to find my footing, probably longer. But one thing I quickly learned was that if you weren't prepared for the 8:15 a.m. meeting, you shouldn't bother attending. Bob always knew the right questions to ask, and I soon realized that he had more knowledge about the economy and monetary policy in his thumb than I had in my brain. He was always a step ahead. You can gauge someone's intelligence not just by their answers, but also by their questions, and after four decades on Bay Street and Wall Street, I can attest that nobody asked tougher or better questions than Bob Brooks. I would stay up late trying to anticipate them. He was always prepared, tough, yet gracious and respectful.

When I moved to New York, I met some of the smartest and most tenacious chief investment officers and business executives in the world: Carl Icahn, Paul Tudor Jones, Bill Gross, Boone Pickens, John Paulson, and many more. After several years of meetings and conferences with these Wall Street titans, I realized that none of them could match Bob Brooks in terms of toughness and smarts. That is the absolute truth. And, most importantly, I always came to meetings with these people exceptionally well-prepared because of Bob.

Bob Brooks had a profound impact on my career, even though we didn't work that closely together. He challenged me in a way that few others have. Everyone I know personally and professionally is aware of Bob Brooks, because I often talk about how influential he was for me. He taught me to anticipate, to be quick on my feet, to leave no stone unturned, and always be prepared. I learned all that from Bob in my late twenties.

Another lesson Bob taught me early on, which I preach to my own staff today, is never bullshit your way through an answer. If you don't know, admit it, but promise to find the answer as soon as possible. In my early days, I tried to baffle Bob with jargon when he asked questions. That didn't go well, and that helped me become a better economist. He was a great teacher who led by example.

While I initially feared him—justifiably so, because he couldn't tolerate people who wasted time—we grew fond of each other through the years. Earning his respect was a badge of honor. Based on the encouraging things he said when I left the Bank in 1994, I knew I had earned it, which meant the world to me.

Later, when I got the top economics job at Merrill Lynch in 2002, Bob invited me to lunch in the Scotiabank executive dining room to celebrate my success. It was a terrific sendoff. I remember thinking, "Is he talking about me?" when I heard the things he said. But Bob never said anything he didn't mean.

I attended Bob's retirement party in late 2008 or early 2009 while I was making my way back to Toronto. We struck up a conversation that seemed to go on for hours. It wasn't about the economy or the markets, but about family, travel, and his plans for the future. Afterward, we decided to have lunch once a quarter. We always went to the same spot: Blowfish for sushi.

Over the next decade, I had the pleasure of getting to know Bob on a personal level. I learned that he had a great sense of humor—he was a brilliant raconteur. We talked about everything from arts to science to sports to world events; there was nothing he couldn't form an informed opinion on.

In my early days at Gluskin Sheff, at one of our lunches, I asked Bob how to make the transition from talking to Merrill Lynch institutional clients to my new firm's retail clients. He said, "Tell them never to put all their eggs in one basket, and that there is never any such thing as a sure thing." If I had a nickel for every time I've used those lines, I'd be retired in Monaco right now.

There's something else about Bob that I think few people are aware of. Over the years, I had the opportunity to meet two Scotiabank CEOs: Peter Godsoe and Rick Waugh. Both said the same thing to me when I mentioned Bob's name as a mentor—that they wouldn't have lasted if it weren't for Bob's wisdom and sage advice. They both said the exact same thing! And in the cutthroat environment that exists in the highest ranks of the banks, this also shows another of Bob's endearing qualities: trust.

I am eternally thankful for having met Bob Brooks, and even more fortunate to have had the opportunity to spend valuable time with him over the years. I miss him dearly and always will. May his memory be a blessing. My prayers are with his family.

* * *

Those who knew Wall Street legend Jack Rivkin will surely agree that he deserves a monument or plaque for radically transforming the investment industry in the 1980s. He shifted it from a male-dominated sector to one where women were finally recognized for their talent, efforts, and achievements. While wage gaps still exist today and need to be resolved, four decades ago, women in finance were expected to be seen but not heard. Jack single-handedly attacked and addressed these prejudices, blazing a trail that few are aware of. This is an attempt to give credit where it is due.

By the time Jack accepted a position at Shearson Lehman in 1987 (the same year I started my career) as head of the firm's fledgling research department, he was already a well-known and successful financial market executive. Even "fledgling" is charitable, as Lehman's research area had been at the bottom of industry rankings for years and was not taken seriously. Jack changed that. He implemented strategic improvements that took Shearson Lehman Brothers from fifteenth in the *Institutional Investor* survey in 1987 to seventh in 1988, fourth in 1989, and to number one in 1990, two years ahead of his schedule. The firm remained at number one for many years under his leadership.

Jack brought discipline and innovative ideas to his new team. One was the introduction of quantitative metrics, which included tracking analysts' rankings, client calls (a minimum of 125 per month), research reports, client inquiries, client visits, and commission revenues generated. He immediately recognized that EQ mattered at least as much as IQ among research analysts, and his implementation of his fabled "no jerk" policy paid dividends from the start. Transparency, accountability, compensation based on teamwork, mentoring, and meritocracy quickly became the norm in a department previously noted for its cozy and, dare I say, lazy culture.

One crucial and, at the time, radical thing that Jack Rivkin did was promote women to leadership positions within research. In fact, it was the first thing he did, helping to eliminate the stifling effects of gender-biased management. When he joined Lehman, he interviewed every member of the research department and quickly realized that the brightest and most ambitious women on staff were being overlooked. That changed rapidly. Male analysts, who were clearly in their roles because of their gender, had female team members in number-two or number-three positions who were more talented and hardworking. Those men were let go, and the yet-to-be-discovered female research analysts were quickly promoted into lead roles. Rivkin already understood what women brought to the table in this alpha-male industry, because when he led the team at Paine Webber, he had promoted Margo Alexander to research director, an unheard-of move at the time.

At Lehman, he instituted a women-friendly environment because he understood that diversity—essential for success in any endeavor and a term now commonly heard at human resource seminars—was crucial, even when it wasn't on anyone else's radar, especially in the investment industry. Try to find a woman on a trading floor in the 1987 movie *Wall Street*. Rivkin found that women in this industry not only offered a unique perspective on problem-solving, but that they were also hungrier, more dedicated, motivated, and hardworking than their male counterparts. They simply had (and still have) something to prove.

It was no coincidence that Lehman topped the rankings by 1990 and that 30 percent of the firm's research department were women, double the industry norm at the time. In fact, 40 percent of his top-ranked analysts were female, triple the standard for the rest of Wall Street. The proof is in the pudding. Rivkin loaded up his department with female research analysts and his group remained top-ranked for years—at least until the rest of Wall Street caught up to his "radical" idea.

I first met Jack in 2003, after moving to New York. He was already chief investment officer of Neuberger Berman, the iconic fund manager. After meeting through George Stephenson, an outstanding Merrill Lynch institutional equity salesperson, Jack and I became quite close. He never missed a presentation I gave to his group, and the three of us had breakfast together quarterly for nearly seven years. I count him among my mentors, not just professionally, but personally.

Sometime in 2005, Candace Browning, then and still head of global research at Bank of America Merrill Lynch, held a leadership symposium at a Midtown hotel. All the heads of the various research units attended, and Candace assigned each of us a different Harvard case study on leadership. We were to read the case thoroughly and present our findings and interpretation in an hour-long dissertation. Candace unknowingly did me a great favor by assigning me Jack's case study. I had no idea what he had accomplished at Shearson Lehman years before, let alone that it was documented in the Harvard Business Review. I devoured the report, and it has stuck with me ever since. A few months later, during breakfast with George and Jack, I told Jack how impactful his experience had been on me. I also asked why he had never mentioned pioneering a "women-friendly environment" in the financial industry. I remember his grin and shrug as he replied, "I don't like to talk about myself," which reminded me that humility was a characteristic he constantly sought in his research team.

I can't recall if I ever thanked Candace for choosing me to lead the discussion on Jack Rivkin at that leadership conference. Nor do I know if I ever adequately thanked my pal George for introducing us and nurturing what became a terrific relationship, one that lasted from 2003 until Jack's passing from pancreatic cancer in November 2016 at the too-young age of seventy-six. Even after I left Wall Street and Jack pursued other endeavors, including a stint with my friends who ran Altegris, we frequently met for "macro/market" idea dinners hosted by Danielle DiMartino and Josh Frankel, not to mention our fishing trips at Camp Kotok in early August. I always admired him and tried to emulate him.

Since meeting Jack Rivkin nearly two decades ago, I have assembled and led teams, and I am proud of their success. I recognized long ago the importance of having a strong contingent of women in senior roles, a realization I may not have fully appreciated without learning from Jack's experience. Looking back at my time at Merrill Lynch and Gluskin Sheff, the women who worked for me have gone on to stellar careers, becoming chief economist of SAC, senior advisor at the Bank of Canada, senior economist at the Oxford Group, and a member of the asset mix committee at the Abu Dhabi sovereign wealth fund, and so on. And without diminishing the contributions of the men on our staff, Rosenberg Research is following in Jack Rivkin's footsteps, with several female stars on the team.

* * *

I credit Gerry Sheff and Ira Gluskin with providing a big assist. After they left their leadership roles, the firm became the Canadian version of *Game of Thrones*. Gerry taught me the art of persuasion, emphasizing how critical it is for a forecaster like myself to convince people (including my team) that my forecast is accurate, and to get buy-in from our partners. That was a valuable lesson, and I thank Gerry for it to this day. He was a visionary. So was Ira, who took that thought to the next level by encouraging me to never say "my forecast" but rather "my base-case forecast," stressing that what is most critical for a wealth manager is how the probabilities of all outcomes are shifting over time. He encouraged me to talk just as much about the risks around my view and in which direction things will go if I am wrong. Gerry taught me about effective communication, while Ira taught me about the effectiveness of scenario building. These were valuable lessons, and it goes to show that at any age, seeking out mentors or role models doesn't go out of style.

I have nothing else to say about my time at Gluskin Sheff, except that the company gave me the opportunity from the start to build a research business within an investment business. As a result, I was able to "stress test" Rosenberg Research years before it was established. By the time I left Gluskin Sheff, I had 1,600 subscribers; today, that number has swelled to 2,300 in more than forty countries.

* * *

Harry Benjamin Rosenberg was my mentor, teacher, and all-around "go-to guy" until he passed from complications from Parkinson's on May 15, 2016.

In 1998, Tom Brokaw published the bestseller *The Greatest Generation* about the generation of heroes from the 1930s and 1940s who endured the Great Depression and the Second World War, and subsequently became great leaders in civilian life. My father belonged to that rare and vanishing breed. He was a true hero—wise, brave, and a man of his word. Of all the people I've met, none possessed a stronger moral compass, and he led by example.

Born in Winnipeg in 1926, Dad was the youngest of eight children. He was raised during the Great Depression. His father died on his fourteenth birthday. His older brothers were fighting in the war, and Dad had to mature quickly, helping to run the household and never really experiencing much of a childhood. I didn't fully appreciate that as a child, but it was a unique learning experience to have a parent who had grown up during the Depression. It wasn't just the frugality, or even the concept of a penny saved is a penny earned—I can still picture Dad scraping the bottom of the peanut butter jar with a spatula or adding a few drops of boiled water to an almost-empty ketchup bottle—but he instilled in me at a young age the feeling that nothing should be taken for granted.

"Waste not, want not" was one of his favorite sayings, and something rarely heard today, but it always resonated with me, as old-fashioned as it sounds. Perhaps that's why I became an economist. The concept of saving for the future was never lost on me, or any of Dad's four children.

Dad's strong moral compass was evident in an incident from my childhood. A developer planned to build a low-income housing project next to our neighborhood, and a petition circulated to stop it. My dad was the only one who didn't sign. I remember him telling us, and I couldn't have been more than six years old, that no one has the right to tell someone else where they are allowed to live. Forty-nine years later, that's what I remember about my dad—a powerful lesson in the fundamental principle of how to treat your neighbor.

Dad once told me his life could have gone either way. Growing up in a rough part of Winnipeg, without a father or older brothers, he lacked a role model. A turning point came when he decided to say Kaddish for his father, as there was no one else to do it. The men at the shul took him under their wing, teaching him Hebrew and how to daven, transforming a directionless ruffian into a mensch. From the age of twelve, he worked constantly, from the nickel and copper mines of northern Alberta to the Canadian National Railway as a cook, funding his education and ultimately earning a master's degree in civil engineering.

A self-made man, he dedicated his professional life to public service, despite more lucrative private sector offers, and rose through the ranks of Environment Canada to lead the government's inland waters directorate. The Great Lakes project, the St. Lawrence Seaway, and the Fraser Valley diversion all bear his mark. In fact, water was a huge passion for Dad. Even as Parkinson's eroded his memory, mentioning "Bruce Heavy Water Plant" would instantly spark his attention, prompting him to recall, eyes closed, "oh yeah, that was 1969." We were probably the only kids on the block who knew the terms "desalination" and "reverse osmosis" by the fourth grade.

Interestingly, Dad's professional life revolved around water, a substance rich with symbolism in Judaism, representing birth, motherhood, and creation. I sometimes wonder if there was a connection between his passion for water and his active shul life in Ottawa. He wasn't just a two-time president of Machzikei Hadas; he understood the importance of community involvement, giving back, and leading by example. He made courageous decisions nearly four decades ago to financially save the shul, never seeking recognition because he embodied humility. As I said, he led by example.

In 1982, Dad and Mom left Canada for Israel, opting to spend their remaining years near their children and grandchildren and travel the world, satisfying their shared curiosity. Dad also consulted part-time and taught math and science to exchange students, reflecting his passion for sharing his vast knowledge and giving back to the community.

My mother passed away in March 2011, and I remember her most for her boundless love. Dad, what he lacked in outward affection, he made up for in wisdom. It was his advice—"sometimes you have to take a step back to take two steps forward"—without which I don't know if I would have embarked on my chosen career path. I still share that story with college graduates, encouraging them to focus not on the dollar but on long-term career paths. Dad applied the same principle to his nearly twenty-five-year battle with Parkinson's disease: one step back, two steps forward. He persevered, adapted to his changing condition, and never complained. He was incredibly brave.

I miss Dad terribly. I remember him as a tremendous success. He lived to eighty-nine, defying expectations, considering his illness. Together, he and Mom raised four wonderful children, had ten grandchildren, and eight great-grandchildren, with more on the way. I know that I wouldn't be the father or man I am today without them.

On a lighter note, I'd like to share a story. In 2003, my first full year at Merrill Lynch in New York, I was asked to be a keynote speaker at the annual CFA dinner at the Sheraton Centre in downtown Toronto. Ira Gluskin was the other speaker that evening. Weeks later, my dad asked me about the event. I told him I spoke about the economic outlook, and Ira presented his new investment idea: income trusts. Dad asked if I could get him a copy of Ira's speech, so I contacted my connections at Gluskin Sheff, who kindly sent it over.

The following Sunday, I visited my parents' condo. I handed Dad Ira's speech, adding, "Here's my speech too, if you're interested." An hour later, I found him at the kitchen table, devouring Mom's famous cheese blintzes while engrossed in Ira's speech. My speech remained untouched on the counter. I asked, "Dad, are you going to read my speech, or just Ira's?" I remember his response vividly. He quipped, "Which speech is going to help me make money, his or yours?"

As I said, Dad was wise.

I began this section with Tom Brokaw's *The Greatest Generation*, and I'll conclude with a similar sentiment. Dad's wisdom was also reflected in his reading choices; he was a voracious reader, but I never saw him pick up a novel. He always chose books on politics, economics, geography, or history. In our house, a long bookcase in the hallway near the front door held classics. I remember noticing a six-volume set of Winston Churchill's memoirs, likely a first edition. As a teenager, I asked Dad if they were his, and he nodded. When I asked if he had read all six volumes, he responded, "Twice!" It's amazing he ever made it to a golf course! He then put his arm around me and said, "Never, never, never give up." I'm struck by the clarity with which I recall that moment, decades later.

CHAPTER 34

Paying It Back

I take great pride in the number of people who walked through my door over the course of my career, and then went on, spread their wings, and experienced successful careers of their own. Here is what I dub the Great Eight (there are many others, but only so much space and time):

Robert Spector, fixed-income portfolio manager at MFS Investment Management
Tom Porcelli, chief economist at Wells Fargo
David Wolf, multi-asset fund manager and portfolio manager at Fidelity
Sheryl King, advisor to the governor at the Bank of Canada
Scott Kinnear, director of financial markets at the Bank of Canada
Neil Dutta, head of economics, Renaissance Macro Research
Drew Matus, chief market strategist, MetLife Investment Management
Ron Wexler, director of business and talent development at NextGen

I have had my share of challenges in my professional life, but the one thing I never suffered was an inability to attract talent. Keeping the talent was another thing altogether, a reflection of their skill sets more than anything else. I definitely had (and still have) a reputation as being a demanding boss, but what is most important in terms of leading a team is (i) being consistent in messaging, (ii) creating a culture of trust and respect, (iii) promoting based purely on merit; (iv) having an open-door policy at all times, (v) never losing your cool and composure, and (vi) sharing the credit when things go right and accepting the blame when things go wrong.

I wish I'd had the benefit of learning from those members as a staff member earlier in my career, but most (not all) of my bosses were low in emotional intelligence. I learned to lead while managing my own teams and by watching leaders I admired. My hope for the folks listed earlier is that as they move into managerial roles, they follow the leadership cues noted earlier—they are what separate a truly effective manager from the pack.

CHAPTER 35

The Fool on the Hill

My Brother Mel teaches an elective class on The Beatles at the University of Tel Aviv. He invited me to one of his podcasts a few years ago and asked me to name my most cherished Beatles song. I told him it was "The Long and Winding Road" (from *Let It Be* in 1970). I always interpreted that phrase "don't leave me waiting here, lead me to your door" as a profoundly personal yearning for that inherently difficult goal of finding your way to the truth and that ever-elusive accurate forecast.

What did you expect? I'm an economist.

After watching the *Beatles Anthology* documentary, and especially the video of Paul, all alone on the top of the hill, looking down as the "Fool on the Hill" was playing, I realized that *it* was my favorite song. The "fool" is not one at all, but rather a wise man mistaken as a "fool" because he is a solitary figure ("alone on a hill") who sees the world differently than everyone else ("nobody ever hears him"). But he is the one on the hill, not the others. He is the one with the big picture sightline while the others only have a linear vision. Late in the song, the tables are turned and you find out who the fools really are.

You can see how this might resonate with someone who has spent much of his career challenging the consensus, the herd mentality, and existing orthodoxy. Only a fool would call a perma bear a fool. As I say over and over, there is little tolerance in the financial industry for those who have a contrary view to the constant bullish narrative. Warren Buffett likes to say that "only when the tide goes out do you discover who's been swimming naked." And the tide does go out—it always goes out. The fact that this bear has survived in the bullring for so long attests to the fact that my team and I are appropriately attired. At the peak of a market bubble, winning means preserving your capital.

Acknowledgments

Throughout this book, I mention many people who inspired me and were instrumental in bolstering my career, as well as my now deceased parents who nourished me and my siblings with love, security, stability, and an emphasis on reading and education.

I had numerous role models along my career path, some are mentioned here, and I apologize to those I may have missed. They include Warren Jestin, Aron Gampel, Michael Shain, Bob Brooks, Don Coxe, Gary Shilling, Richard Bernstein, Lacy Hunt, Jack Rivkin, Doug Behnfield, Jeff Burchell, Michael Isenberg, Brahm Satov, Gerry Sheff, and, of course, Bob Farrell.

In addition to the other mentors I mention in these pages, I'd like to add my older brother Mel, a renowned scientist, inventor, musician, and author. He was a significant inspiration for this book. He has just published a children's novel entitled *Emily Saw a Door*—it is creative and sensational. He did this just as he was turning seventy-four, so I thought it was time I got going on my book, although I'm not sure it will gain the same audience.

I also want to thank my two sisters, Miriam and Rena. Without their tutelage in my younger years, I most assuredly would never have made it past grade school.

I paid tribute earlier to the many role models I've had in my long career, but there is one individual who may be the best market economist I have ever met in my life, Ken Bercuson, who worked on the trading desk in my days at Merrill in New York and went on to have a storied career at a hedge fund. Ken is now retired, but he had such a major influence on how to step up my game that he is an advisor to Rosenberg Research and we talk frequently.

My trainer and "ambassador of kwan" for these past fifteen years, Sean Trotman, deserves a tip of the hat for keeping me in at least respectable physical condition.

My dear friend, Richard Yamarone, was my confidante extraordinaire and alter ego for many years. May he rest in peace after an untimely and tragic death in November 2017.

My son Jacob helped me build my business to where it is today and is our de facto chief operating officer. Not even thirty years old yet, he has emerged as a true visionary and a leader of the firm.

Jacob is the middle of three sons. The eldest is Daniel, a physician. The baby, twenty-six-year-old Michael, is pursuing a career in hospitality. While there is no diversification in terms of gender, I most certainly am diversified with regard to the non-correlated nature of their professions.

And finally, my wife, Rachael. She has also been instrumental in the business. Not only does she handle all the thankless but essential back-office stuff, but her dedication and attention spent on our three sons allowed me to chase my career all these years. That is one of the things people have to know in order to succeed in their personal and business lives. The higher you go, the more elusive a work-life balance becomes. It is vital to marry someone who is aligned with you with regard to career goals, particularly in the financial services sector. Rachael sacrificed a lot. She deserves a ton of credit for allowing me the time to pursue a career I could have only dreamed of in my younger years. She has been a constant source of encouragement and my best advisor in all things related to life and business. I should add that Rachael started out her career as a social worker before deciding that raising the boys and nurturing a warm home was paramount. I tell people I was her first and last patient.

About the Author

David Rosenberg is a renowned global economist and financial market strategist with four decades of experience spanning Wall Street and Bay Street. During his ten years at Merrill Lynch, he consistently ranked as an all-star in the Brendan Wood and *Institutional Investor* client surveys. David has played a crucial role in his career shaping public opinion on the investment landscape and providing investors with a differentiated and unique lens not found through other channels in the financial forecasting industry.

He has spent his career successfully placing bets against the consensus opinion and has never been one to follow the herd. Capital preservation and focusing on safety and income at a reasonable price have been his mantra. Investors who heeded his advice to reduce risk ahead of the bubble busts of 2000 and 2008 emerged unscathed.

In 2020, David started his own research consulting business, Rosenberg Research. He caters to thousands of retail and institutional clients in more than forty countries. The breadth of his research mirrors that of his broad and diversified customer base. His long-standing *Breakfast with Dave* publication is a must-read for investors around the world. He is a sought-after speaker at financial and business events and is a frequent guest on television, radio, and an array of social media platforms.